Amin's Soldiers

A Caricature of Upper Prison

John Pancras Orau

Amin's Soldiers
A Caricature of Upper Prison
John Pancras Orau

ISBN 978-1-904380-96-2 (Paperback)
ISBN 978-1-908162-46-5 (Adobe E-book)
ISBN 978-1-908162-47-2 (Kindle /Epub E-book)

Copyright © 2013 This work is the copyright of John Pancras Orau. All intellectual property and associated rights are hereby asserted and reserved by the author in full compliance with UK, European and international law. No part of this book may be copied, reproduced, stored in any retrieval system or transmitted in any form or by any means, including in hard copy or via the internet, without the prior written permission of the publishers to whom all such rights have been assigned worldwide.

Cover design © 2013 Waterside Press. Design by www.gibgob.com

Cataloguing-In-Publication Data A catalogue record for this book can be obtained from the British Library.

e-book *Amin's Soldiers* is available as an ebook and also to subscribers of Myilibrary, Dawsonera, ebrary and Ebscohost.

Printed by Lightning Source, Milton Keynes.

Main UK distributor Gardners Books, 1 Whittle Drive, Eastbourne, East Sussex, BN23 6QH. Tel: +44 (0)1323 521777; sales@gardners.com; www.gardners.com

USA and Canada distributor Ingram Book Company, One Ingram Blvd, La Vergne, TN 37086, USA. (800) 937-8000, orders@ingrambook.com, ipage.ingrambook.com

Published 2013 by
Waterside Press Ltd.
Sherfield Gables
Sherfield on Loddon
Hook, Hampshire
United Kingdom RG27 0JG

Telephone +44(0)1256 882250
E-mail enquiries@watersidepress.co.uk
Online catalogue WatersidePress.co.uk

Amin's Soldiers

A Caricature of Upper Prison

John Pancras Orau

≫ WATERSIDE PRESS

'The last time I saw John Orau he was sitting in his tiny bookshop in Uganda wiling away his time reading. I asked how many he had sold today.
He thought hard then answered, "None".
"And yesterday?"
"None, either".
He was writing this book and his only ambition was to one day see it in print':

Reverend Gordon Randall.

TABLE OF CONTENTS

The Author	vi
Idi Amin Dada: Publisher's Note	vii
Acknowledgements	ix
Preface	x
Dedication	xv
Glossary	xvi
1. **Arrest!**	19
2. **Some Even More Bizarre Travels to Prison**	27
3. **Flashback**	33
4. **Salad Days**	43
5. **Journal of a Salad Day**	69
6. **Hunger Amid Hope**	81
7. **Hunger, Hunger — Amid Suspense**	103
8. **Days of Plenty**	119
9. **We Make Life Gay**	137
10. **Fast Bind, Fast Find**	145
11. **Latter Days**	163
12. **Final Days**	177
Epilogue	183
Index	185

THE AUTHOR

John Pancras Orau was born in Pallisa, Eastern Uganda, in 1949, where he attended Kamuge'linga Primary School and St Pius X Minor Seminary, Nagongera, Tororo. He went on to Katigondo Major Seminary in Masaka, Southern Uganda, but soon quit priestly training to join the Ugandan Air Force. Grounded in the early stages of flight training, he transferred to the Operations Office of the Air Force Communications Department.

As President Idi Amin was swept from power and in common with thousands of existing service personnel, his career was cut short. After more than two years incarcerated in Upper Prison, he eventually found work on the shop floor of Uganda's *New Vision* daily newspaper. An 'avid and omnivorous' reader he is now retired and lives once again in his home town of Pallisa.

John Pancras Orau

IDI AMIN DADA: PUBLISHER'S NOTE

JOHN ORAU TOUCHES ON the regime of Idi Amin at several places in this book, which forms the backdrop to the story he has to tell. Modern generations might not immediately recognise the eccentric Ugandan dictator, whilst older generations may appreciate a brief refresher.

Idi Amin was born in the 1920s (exactly when remains a mystery). He was amongst the most flamboyant of world leaders and, to western eyes, one of the most notorious, tyrannical and provocative. The third President of Uganda from 1971 to 1979 following independence, he had earlier attained the rank of Major-General under British rule after joining the army as an assistant cook without qualifications. He later rose to be Commander-in-Chief of the post-colonial Ugandan armed forces. Subsequently reduced to being in charge of the army only, he seized power in 1971 in a military coup from President Milton Obote, the very person who had demoted him.

Given to pageantry, ceremony and display, in which he mimicked the British[1] whilst mixing this with African rites and rituals, he proclaimed himself:

> His Excellency President for Life, Field Marshal Alhaji Dr. Idi Amin Dada, VC, DSO, MC, CBE, Lord of All the Beasts of the Earth and Fishes of the Seas, King of Scotland.[2]

His military rule was characterised by abuse, persecution, corruption, brinkmanship, unpredictability and fragile international allegiances. Estimates put the number of his own people killed during his time in power at from 100,000 to 500,000 (including opponents who simply "disappeared").[3]

Amongst high profile events, the wholesale expulsion of Ugandan Asians in 1972 ranks high on the barometer of abuses (one of the largest business groups they were targeted in Amin's "Economic War") whilst that at Entebbe

---

1. As when awarding himself the Victorious Cross (VC), a medal emulating the British Victoria Cross and styling himself Conqueror of the British Empire (CBE).
2. Hence the 2006 biopic *The Last King of Scotland* for which the American actor Forest Whitaker as Amin won an Academy Award. Amin's title sometimes varied with the occasion.
3.. One apocryphal tale is that he kept their heads in the fridge; but this may just be propaganda. John Orau describes some of Amin's actual reprisals against opponents in *Chapter 3*.

Airport in 1976 was also highly visible internationally. In the latter incident, Amin allowed an Air France airliner hijacked principally by the Popular Front for the Liberation of Palestine to land in Uganda. Some 150 non-Jewish hostages were released whilst over 80 Jews and Israeli citizens (as well as 20 others including the captain and crew) remained hostage. In a surprise mission, Israeli commandos struck in what became known as "The Raid on Entebbe". Several passengers died or were wounded; and seven hijackers, 45 Ugandan soldiers and one Israeli commando were killed.

Despite many reported atrocities, Amin's singular stand against the West led to his election as chair of the Organization of African Unity and helped him to forge alliances with the UK's then Cold War enemies, notably Russia and East Germany. All of this led to Great Britain cutting off relations with Uganda in 1977.

Long before the age of "social media", Amin's regime was brought down by his growing reputation at home for human rights abuses, personal excess and ill-advised military outings, culminating in the Uganda-Tanzania War. It is the end of that war which forms the immediate background to this book. Amin fled to Colonel Gaddafi's Libya then to Saudi Arabia where, free from investigation for crimes against humanity, he died in 2003.

Notable traits of Idi Amin were his huge physical presence and deceptive charm. He was Ugandan light heavyweight boxing champion from 1951 to 1960, a strong swimmer and a powerful rugby player, though a colleague once described him as being "bone from the neck up". That is certainly how he was viewed in the west: a buffoon, a loose cannon, a "gentle giant" suffering from delusions of grandeur. There are those who criticise the west for allowing the comic book nature of his profile to mask the extent of his abuses.

"Amin's soldiers" became a term of derision for those who had served and fought under him (and who he finally walked out on as his regime crumbled), but who, at the time, as John Orau describes in this telling book, believed that they were serving their country as loyalty dictated. What happened next is the subject of this rare inside account.

ACKNOWLEDGEMENTS

I am grateful to Dr Otim P. Charles from whom came the suggestion and exhortation to write this book, and who would in the end lend a hand in e-correspondence with the agent and the publisher in "mid-wiving" the birth of the book; to Mr Bigo Nyarubona (RIP), whose tip I found worth its weight in gold; and to my Helvetian friend Mr Markus Hess, a one-time International Committee of the Red Cross (ICRC) delegate in Kampala, whose favour enabled the typing of the manuscript. And, finally, I can never adequately thank the Reverend Gordon Randall and Canon Keith Price and the Eastleigh Bukedi Link,[4] without whose help and clout this book would probably never have seen the light of day at all.

---

4. The Anglican Diocese of Winchester has been linked with the Church of Uganda since 1977. Eastleigh Deanery (a group of parishes within the Diocese of Winchester) is linked with the Ugandan Diocese of Bukedi and it is through this connection that the manuscript of this book found its way to England.

PREFACE

IN APRIL 1979, UGANDA's standing army, under the leadership of cut-throat dictator and self-styled Life President Field Marshal Idi Amin, was routed and put to flight. In the course of liberating Uganda from his unremitting eight-year rule of terror and murder, the juggernaut of liberation contingents from south-neighbouring Tanzania was spearheaded by the Tanzania People's Defence Force (TPDF).

There was, of course, a Ugandan constituent, too, of about 20 fragmented factions of anti-Amin dissident exiles, who fought under the umbrella of the Uganda National Liberation Front (UNLF) or Army (UNLA), the political and military complements of the movement.

Vicious consequences were meted out to the remaining 6,000 or so soldiers (by no means the rump of the Ugandan Army), who were blameless, even if they might be seen as a menace to peace and security. They were confined and kept hungry in Luzira and other prisons where they languished under the rudest oppression and humiliation for two years-plus in dehumanising and privative conditions.

Comparatively, however, the experience may not have been all that harrowing, much less horrifying. But so bizarre, so larger-than-life was it that I'm not likely to forget it soon. Two years in prison is more than my fair share of trouble.

This episode is yet another significant page—and "missing link"—in Uganda's turbulent history and it can't just go untold, even though it may be argued in some quarters that it is a mere footnote in history!

The events and changes of the immediate post-Amin era took place amid a state of severe insecurity—characterised by wanton killing and plunder (by who else than yesterday's "Knights in Shining Armour"?!), random battles, personal vendettas, armed robberies and political intimidation in a ruthless man-eat-man power struggle. Yet another sad chapter in the annals of Uganda.

In just around one-and-a-half-years, the presidency changed hands a record four times, eventually re-instating, in the long-promised and long-awaited elections, that headstrong demagogue with an extraordinary gift of the gab and sense of humour, Dr. Apolo Milton Obote, whom Amin—undoubtedly Obote's own version of Frankenstein's monster—had toppled and forced into exile in his bloody military coup of 1971. (But that, for sure, is far from saying that Uganda's chapter of accidents had come to an end. Regrettably, it would still remain perennially at war and strife with itself and, eventually, Obote was also to become the first president to be deposed by a military uprising a *second* time!).

The label "Amin's soldiers" (which seems to be a permanent stigma upon us, although we ourselves cannot own-up to being ashamed of ourselves) is improper and obnoxious to my former colleagues and me but by using it as the title of this book I want to dispel this. I could not help adopting the misnomer, if only for the sake of distinguishing our lot from the liberating contingents or the New Ugandan Army. Any offence is regretted.

All the names of the *dramatis personae* in this prison melodrama have been changed in order to protect identities, as far as that is possible. But there has been no attempt whatever to disguise the names and identities of presidents, past and present, as they would still stand out a mile in any case. Any inconvenience here is regretted. And uncomplimentary comments about them, if any, are also regretted.

The chronological sequence of events in this story may be slightly flawed here and there, whilst some of the dialogues herein may not be one hundred per cent true to the original. The reason is that I had to reconstruct and improvise these in cases of partial or total lapse of memory while I was piecing this memoir together.

Likewise, any other remarks (in direct or indirect speech) ascribed, e.g. to visiting Cabinet ministers, Members of Parliament, clergymen and other bigwigs may not be verbatim or entirely conform to standards of "journalistic accuracy and credibility": There was neither a voice-recording device to hand nor any on-the-spot possibility of copying them into writing. I did, however, record salient points by rote and have reproduced what I believe is a fair portrayal of what was uttered and meant.

In one case only—in *Chapter 5*—I've had to resort dramatic licence, sometimes weaving together notable events and snippets from different days of our waking hours and crowding them all into a single day's journal.

I also take this opportunity, on my and the other inmates' behalf, to express our gratitude to the delegates of the International Committee of the Red Cross, whose errands of mercy so much lightened the weight of our own cross on the long arduous journey and ordeal to our freedom, and who might also, one way or another, have been instrumental in making our releases occur sooner rather than later (or perhaps never?).

Similarly, to my own kith and kin who sustained me materially, morally and otherwise, during yet another ordeal, that of writing this volume (whether they were aware that I was doing it or not), I am ever more than obliged.

But, still, I owe this book more to the long while of unemployment that I found myself in after leaving prison, such idleness that, ironically, gave way to this literary toil!

John Pancras Orau
Kamuge'linga
Pallisa
June 2013

They that be slain with the sword
are better than they that be slain with hunger:
For these pine away stricken through
for want of the fruits of the field.

                                      Lamentations 4:9

DEDICATION

To Daughter Susan Kateme.

To Uncle Silver Ochola.

And to the Memory of my Old-time Friends and Colleagues of the air and ground crew of the defunct Uganda Air Force, living and deceased.

GLOSSARY

Foreign words are Swahili unless indicated

Afende A title used by soldiers to address their superiors.
Alur (plural the same) An ethnic group on the western side of downstream River Nile in a region generally called West Nile.
Askari A soldier or guard.
Balking Thwarting, stopping, getting in the way.
Bazungu See Mzungu.
Bootless In vain.
Buganda See Muganda.
Bei laisi A bargain, something going cheap.
Bhang A drink or meal prepared from the leaves and flowers of cannabis plants.
BVM Blessed Virgin Mary.
Choo Loo, toilet.
Coif Veil.
Continentals Europeans.
DP Democratic Party.
Enguli Variant of Waragi (see below), in the crude form only.
Etesot (plural Iteso) An ethnic group in eastern Uganda.
Gomesi (Bantu) Traditional women's short-sleeved, elaborate, ankle length dress.
In iming (Luo) You are stupid.
Kanzu (Bantu) Traditional cassock (usually white).
Karibu Ndugu Welcome brother.
Kopolo The local corruption of corporal.
Mabus Jail.
Madaraka Tricks.
Malaya Harlot.
Malwa (Bantu) A native beer concocted from millet as the main ingredient.
Magendoists Black marketeers.
Matoke Cooked bananas as a meal.
Muchomo Roast meat.

Muganda An inhabitant of Buganda, the largest ethnic group in Uganda.

Mukiga (plural Bakiga) An ethnic group in the hilly terrain of western Uganda called Kigezi.

Musoga (plural Basoga) An ethnic group of Uganda on the eastern side of the source of the River Nile, a region generally called Busoga.

Mzungu (Bazungu) A neither derogatory nor complimentary word for white person, or, e.g. a white organization such as the Red Cross *Bazungu* in *Chapter 4*.

Pelf Contemptuous word for money or wealth, especially when ill-gotten.

Shriving Confession.

Slugabed A person who delays getting out of bed, out of sleepiness or laziness (A blend of slug(gard) plus abed).

Sokoni Open-air market.

Sufuria Saucepan.

Taarab Type of music with an Arabic character, popular on the East African Coast.

Taba Unprocessed tobacco leaf.

Tamping Prodding, stirring, mixing.

Ten cells system That under which for every ten households, there is one democratically elected leader; and so on upwards through hamlets and villages.

Ugali Bread made from maize flour.

Unga Maize flour.

UNLA Uganda National Liberation Army (recruits).

UPC Uganda People's Congress.

Wananchi Citizens.

Waragi Either the distilled (licensed) or the (unlicensed) form of Uganda's native gin made from either cassava or maize or banana or molasses as main ingredients.

Amin's Soldiers

CHAPTER ONE

ARREST!

Thousands of us were lured into jails, only to take the rap for basically the faults of so few: Obote and Amin.

WITH THE CAPTURE OF the capital city, Kampala, on the 11th of April 1979, the liberation war had virtually come to an end, with only mopping-up operations still going on. The political wing of the Uganda National Liberation Front (UNLF) had now come to the forefront in full play. The politicians, old-time and emergent alike, first and foremost began to share out among themselves the spoils of the Cabinet as the militant wing too had done with other kinds of booty.

One Professor Yusuf Lule, until then little-known on the political stage, was proclaimed president by diktat; an interim Parliament known as the National Consultative Council (NCC) was launched (whose members were merely nominated or cherry-picked, based, of course, mostly on the spoils system and loyalties). So began yet another era of false hope, with illusions of peace and security, and hollow promises of no victimisation, social justice, and fair elections — promises of Utopia! And amid the alliterative rallying cry "Reconstruction, Rehabilitation, Reconciliation", 13 million Ugandans rejoiced and celebrated in a wild euphoria!

One of the top priorities of the new Government's recovery programme was to redress the future composition of the new national army by ensuring equitable recruitment and representation of all tribes in an army of "young, educated Ugandan nationals". They would be politicised, another novel idea, to distinguish them from Amin's army of unschooled goons (as they would have them all to be), and thus put them (Amin's soldiers) to utter shame.

Meanwhile, as soon as Kampala had been liberated, the hunt for Amin's fugitive soldiers got seriously under way everywhere in the country. The unluckiest ones were lynched by rampaging, fanatical, demonstrating mobs or shot dead by the UNLF men in mopping-up operations. No doubt, then, that such persecution and hounding, amid wild rumours of impending, calculated vengeance, made the most desperate ones commit suicide to avoid that "fearful" fate. And, with fresh memories of the spine-chilling atrocities that occurred during Amin's *coup d'etat* only eight years gone by, who could blame them?

Yet, at the same time, a Government spokesman had broadcast assurances to the effect that they (the new Government) wanted all Amin's soldiers alive and that if only they (Amin's soldiers) would surrender, they could then be integrated into the ranks of the new liberation army to help maintain security. That might have been expected and thought to be realistic, for how could the Government otherwise ignore and let be at large about 6,000 soldiers under arms?

The bulk of Amin's army, about 15,000-strong, for fear of reprisals, had retreated in disarray behind the frontiers, in neighbouring Sudan, Zaire[1] and Kenya, where some of them might have roots; so the Government did not have to worry about them. At least for the time being they posed no military threat.

Of course, it was not easy to guess what the Government's unilateral olive branch was all about. Happily, it could turn out to be an honest, well-meaning conciliatory experiment; but unhappily, too, it could be the bait for some punitive agenda. All the same, the unsuspecting April fools acted at the earliest opportunity. Obligingly, they did as directed: They surrendered their weapons to police and military bases. Disarmed and most of them de-uniformed, they were transported to Kampala from their respective districts and herded into Makindye Military Prison barracks. A last-ditch warning that those who did not respond to this amnesty offer would be regarded as and dealt with as rebels, obliged many more to give themselves up.

For my own part, I was sceptical about the Government's intention, so I was loth to go at first. But when I heard that most of my colleagues had returned and were still returning, I weighed the crucial question: "To go or not to go?" I decided that the rule of thumb was to throw in my lot with the multitude, to jump on the bandwagon that is. (After all, isn't there a saying

---

1. So named by its former dictator, the late Mobutu Tseseseko, but which has now reverted to its original name of Congo.

that there is safety in numbers?) So I elected to go with them and foolhardily I travelled to Kampala in early-May. Even more remnants of Amin's soldiers were compelled to follow suit later by the new kind of grass roots regimentation, which did not leave them at peace in their refuges either. The witch-hunting "ten cells" system[2] left almost no loopholes for fugitives or strangers. At least that was the impression at first.

I arrived at Makindye at sunset and found there were already hundreds of my former colleagues there, who for about the past three weeks had been arriving from every part of the country. Our reunion was marked with a revived morale and camaraderie. Fresh arrivals were received fondly with bear hugs, elaborate handshakes and other forms of welcome accompanied indeed with effusive babble and gales of laughter. I overheard it said in jest that surely the war had been better lost than won, so that we too could have been liberated. There was no talk, no sign whatsoever of foreboding for what lay in store for us — nothing to betray the secret behind our being at this place.

Makindye Prison, about three miles to the south of Kampala, was commandeered from the quasi-autonomous Buganda Kingdom — an almost aloof partner with its own Parliament (*Lukiiko*) in the then semi-federal system — after the ouster of King Frederick Edward Mutesa II. It became the location of the headquarters of the military police, where some of Amin's political foes (real or imagined) were liquidated or tortured. Unlike most other suburbs, it has pleasant, "posh" surroundings. A chain-link fence encloses its barracks area, which has a few storeyed blocks of flats and other types of inferior buildings for the jailers to live in, and a large expanse of playgrounds. This prison, once described in some horror stories as the "Black Hole of Kampala", has a small number of dungeons which may keep only a couple of hundred prisoners. Naturally, they could not keep our large number inside there even had they so wished.

We were left at liberty and at will. We were even permitted to go out and come back as and when we pleased, provided curfew time was observed. Our Tanzanian sentries would merely caution us in an I-don't-care attitude: "If you go away, you will be arrested or even killed at the road blocks". They were certain we had no identity documents to enable us pass through these.

---

2. See the *Glossary*.

Always, one meagre meal was provided to last a whole day, and it took several hours to be distributed to a seemingly endless queue. Those, however, who could afford it were able to go out to buy supplements from the streets.

Most of us had come without any blankets, bedsheets or extra clothes, none of which we could find in the prison, let alone beds and mattresses. The early comers, however, had found and salvaged abandoned uniforms, not excluding those warm, heavy army greatcoats, women's clothes, canvas cloths, discarded rags and empty paper boxes, with which they improvised as their bedding. Without such trash, unless you had brought your own bedding, you would have to sleep in your day clothes on the bare concrete floor. Most of us, without extra clothes to wear, could not change in a long, long time. But we were always able to take showers, using a short supply of soap borrowed among ourselves.

We were willing to suffer these privations on the understanding and in the hope that we would soon be quitting them for normal life back in the army. The prospect of a longer sojourn here could have given some of us a mind to decamp.

Every morning, a short-bearded Ugandan captain would come to muster us on the playground to reassure us. On this particular morning, the 12th of May 1979, he came to us as usual and, as he always did, chanted some slogans for the liberation and the president, and we, as required, chorused them after him. Then he announced that some top brass officers were due to address us after his departure. It was then that buses began arriving and parking at the gate, one after another.

The officers we were expecting, so it turned out, were the Commissioner of Prisons and an *aide-de-camp*. They arrived shortly after the captain had departed, and we were again rallied to hear them out.

After a salutation and preamble, the commissioner, smiling with a prepossessing, friendly quality, went on to tell us that it was now necessary to move us out of Makindye. As our number had swollen and we were becoming too congested, and what with the scarce food at Makindye, his argument was plausible.

"So," he went on, "accommodation has been arranged for you in Luzira, with more and better food…"

He waited for the point to sink home and then, reading quizzical and suspicious expressions on some faces, he continued with his spiel.

"You will be there for only a few more days while you await orders for your new deployment…"

He was so cunningly vague and careful not to mention the word "prison", which probably was why most of us were made to presume that we were going to be billeted at Luzuria in the jailers' quarters as we were in Makindye. The more so was this conviction enhanced when he exhorted, "Come on, the earlier you go, the better the chances of finding beds and mattresses". His style and manner inspired such confidence that we could just as well have believed that he was inviting us to go on a picnic outing.

Thereupon, the crowd dispersed promptly and followed the officers to an office by the gate (known in military parlance as quarter guard). Those who had pieces of luggage to pick up were scurrying to the barrack rooms for them in a frenzy. Strangely enough, despite the promise of beds and mattresses, even the trash owners retrieved their bits and pieces and carried them under their arms, looking for all the world like homeless tramps.

We stood before the officers again in two long queues, and they took down our names before we boarded the waiting Tanzanian buses. We were then conducted to them. They had stickers plastered on them proclaiming *kamata yeye* (catch 'em), which was a sufficient tell tale sign! Two armed escorts were posted in each bus. At the gate women and men had gathered since early morning to see their husbands or relatives, as the case might be, but had been refused permission to do so. The reason was obvious: They could have leaked out what lay in store for us. The buses drove out of the gate one after another as they looked on and waved to us in the silent gloom.

We drove along the city thoroughfares, where onlookers took to the streets to tease and jeer at us. Some of the bystanders acted out pantomimes that made us understand we were heading for our doom. They probably knew it as a matter of fact.

Along the rest of the journey, whenever the bus slowed down to a near halt amid heavy traffic, we were subjected to similar teasing, insults, threats and all sorts of imprecations from yet more spontaneous demonstrators, evidently gloating over the prospect of us getting our comeuppance. We were at last relieved of them when the bus branched off to a less used road, then accelerated towards our destination.

Strange as it might seem, it had not occurred to most, if not all, of us yet that mortal vengeance or some other kind of retribution could be the very motive of the process we were involved in right now. Perhaps the real culprits had got away with impunity, but we the remnants were the handiest victims that could serve to appease the enemy's passion for revenge. After all, "vengeance is at least human", to quote George Bernard Shaw.

Now there were murmured conversations of misgivings, as a vague apprehension began to dawn on us. Someone on the next seat asked another man, "Don't you think we are being lured to be shut in prison?"

"No," replied the other, still banking on an earlier assurance, "we are going to be there only a few short days and they will then send us back to work. *Wanawezi kufunga sisi ndani ya mabus kwa seksen gani?* (Under what section or provision of the law can they lock us up in prison?) What had we done to be condemned to imprisonment? *Was that really the price to pay for serving in the legitimate armed forces of our mother Uganda?*"

Now, after all that happened, I do not believe that our term in prison and subsequent disbandment (with no gratuity, no pension whatever to set us up for life) was a spontaneous affair. I am inclined to believe instead that it was schemed with malice intended by those who charted the course of the liberation at the Moshi conference table (for Moshi is the Tanzanian town where the military and political alliance against Amin was hatched with the then famous slogan "Moshi Spirit"). Yet, in fairness, this radical expedient was a judicious and perhaps the only pragmatic course of action; for it is now hard to think that Amin's soldiers, let loose or promptly recalled to the army, could have co-existed with the very people they had been at war with without problems of a considerable magnitude. Moreover, within the loose coalition of UNLF factions themselves, there were internecine feuds fuelled mostly by an overambitious scramble for power, suspicion and profound distrust of one another.

Amin's soldiers could only have compounded the problems of the divisive UNLF. And, in spite of myself, I may also justify this course of action from a historical precedent: I learnt that German soldiers were also confined in their own jails after the liberation of Europe in World War II.

But most of us could not help thinking that we were gullible noodles in regard to the way we had been tricked and lured into prison without an ounce of coercion. I reckon those prison officers must have been congratulated for their cunning. We had swallowed the bait, hook, line and sinker; such was the height of our folly that even if they had invited us to go one mile, we would have gone two. Yet, and still not lost from memory, that was more or less the manner in which some gormless victims of the 1971 coup were baited, only to be decimated.

The bus ride brought us to the main gate of the Luzira Prison complex. We stopped before it, and one of the escorts got out to explain his mission to the gatekeeper. Soon the gate swung wide open and we drove on up the steep rise of a meandering avenue to the threshold of Upper Prison.

The bus stood there for some moments as we stared at the imposing classical facade over the entrance to this prison before getting out. To this facade the sign writer might have ascribed the emblem of the skull and crossbones to bespeak the obvious dangers behind it; but instead it was graced by the comely bright maroon banner of the Uganda Prison Service, belying the ugly existence within. Upon it too was a slab with Roman numerals suggesting that Upper Prison had just marked its golden jubilee! We got out in no hurry and stood there idly for a few moments before the portal was thrown wide open from within and we were invited to step inside, and there was no impolite language.

As soon as we were all herded into the large reception lobby, the huge door was swung shut behind us. The hitherto polite language had been shut out too. We were received by a host of over-zealous prison warders, who now conducted us with peremptory orders, to our bafflement:

"Stand in four rows... Down on your haunches..."

If you demurred or hesitated to respond, a heavy truncheon might crash mercilessly on you. These men were a real match for the savage criminals they usually kept! Quickly we grasped the new situation and were obeying their imperatives with military punctuality and precision.

Our names were recorded as we sat down in tandem in four rows, and a head count took place. But we were not searched or deprived of anything, which ignores standard procedure in prison: your clothes, sandals, money and other personal effects are usually left in the charge of the reception clerk, and you change into a prisoner's uniform at once.

At a command we stood up and, in the wake of a warder, stepped out of the reception hall through another two equally large portals into an expansive quadrangle. There, in the midst of it, we stopped briefly and the warder told us to make ourselves at home. Quietly, dispiritedly, we dispersed.

Other busloads of prisoners were received in the same manner, batch after batch. By sunset of that same day, as more and more prisoners arrived not only from Makindye but also from other places, we should have repented of our folly. How long we were going to be there, only Heaven knew!

As the warder had just told us to, we tried to make ourselves at home. We occupied cells at will and gathered up whatever amenities and creature comforts we could find: just aluminium bowls, tin mugs and a few straw mats! That night, after eating supper of half-baked *ugali* and tough beans (moreover we had to scramble for it in the dim twilight), the warders forcibly pushed and locked us inside the cells amid angry protests and vile abuse from ourselves. Again, we laid our bones to rest for the umpteenth time on the hard, bare concrete floor. Moreover it was infested with lice and a far cry from the utterances of that accursed, lying commissioner!

CHAPTER TWO

SOME EVEN MORE BIZARRE TRAVELS TO PRISON

I really wonder if, in the records of history, any sane man, of his own free will, ever walked, nay argued his way, into prison!

During the several weeks that followed, Upper Prison continued to take in large numbers of prisoners daily. So too, as I learnt, did other prisons all over the country. When we arrived we found hardly a soul, how come? On their arrival at our own and other prisons, the Tanzanians "liberated" the prisoners, presuming them all to have been Amin's unjustified hostages. Thus Uganda's rankest criminal convicts—even lifers and gallows-birds—were all unleashed in one go—along, of course, with other innocent victims, only to make room for Amin's soldiers and so-called henchmen (or was it hatchet men?). It was soon rumoured that some of those criminals had somehow acquired guns from the flotsam of firearms occasioned by the war, only to kill and rob again, thus compounding insecurity in the country.

As droves of prisoners were being brought in daily, in less than two weeks our number had by far exceeded what the prison should hold and still abide by public health ordinances: 600 prisoners only. The manner of arrest and delivery to Upper Prison typified the whole by our capture, arrival and reception as narrated in the preceding chapter. There were, however, exclusive circumstances in and methods by which some other prisoners were taken or lured into prison (which I shall relate shortly).

While we licked our wounds, we discussed the travails of the war and carried out a critical postmortem on it; we had a denunciatory review of Amin's misrule, at which false swearers were heard anxiously and vehemently disowning Amin "before the cock crows". Besides discussing the inevitable weather, we exchanged shoptalk; we discussed our families and other beloved ones. (And, of course, among soldiers, especially, a raunchy topic could never fail to crop up, I need hardly say.) We told and listened to folklore and endless old wives' tales. And there was a host of stories of peculiar arrests of certain people. I was an active gadabout with an ear to the ground, nosing around and with a bit of a roving eye, so I got rewarded with the following earfuls:

The Unlucky Number

Thirteen prisoners, sent directly from a distant up-country police cell, had arrived here three days earlier. One of them told me that they had found the prison devoid of any form of life except, of course, the omnipresent lice (their name is legion!) and various kinds of vermin, and that the prison had been as silent as the graveyard. They had lived in the desolate conditions they had found there and been provided with no food until our arrival three days later.

Later on, there was a rumour (jocular or not) that those early comers had preyed on a whole tribe of cats that once roamed the prison compounds, as they could find no other delicacy in the prison. When I sought to verify this allegation, I found out instead an argument and conclusion that, if the prison had been keeping such pets, those poor creatures might have been so preyed on by Amin's prisoners and not by Amin's soldiers. This is the more logical assumption, since Amin's prisoners, deprived of food, were virtually deserted a good many days before his fall.

Major Michelin

Among our lot there happened to be an exceedingly fat major who, in a manner of speaking, looked as though he were an incarnation of Michelin Man, the trade mark of the French tyre company. Such obesity must have been the result of gourmandising on the finest food and beverages from the officers' mess and canteen for the previous score of years or so.

As I learnt, he was smartly dressed in an expensive suit, carrying a fine brief case, yet another vogue symbol of his exalted status. So he arrived in Kampala, to be received by his Tanzanian counterparts in the stately Nile Mansion, which was their makeshift headquarters at the time. Having introduced himself, he was entertained all afternoon in a most friendly atmosphere. As they fraternised, they hob-nobbed and dined and supped on excellent food and whisky until the curfew hour drew near. Little did the major know that his next good food and wine would come in two long years!

With suave courtesy he was proffered a lift to his "quarters" for the night. The major, of course, thought he was going to be chauffeured to some luxurious lodge or rest house, where he would still slumber in style and comfort. As may well be assumed, in the tradition of VIP protocol, the major rode in the back seat — "assassination corner" — until they arrived at the door of Upper Prison. The major, to his consternation, had become a pariah in a sudden caprice of fate.

Some Argued Their Way In

Like the unlucky 13 prisoners, many other herds of prisoners were taken directly to Upper Prison from various police stations and military outposts, where they had been kept in temporary custody. But some other prisoners made the journey to Kampala under their own steam. In Kampala, when they heard that their colleagues were in Luzira, they set forth unescorted. Some young officers drove there in a family car and literally argued their way in.

"But we were told to report here," they protested to the puzzled and reluctant turnkey.

When the door yielded for them to enter, they blew cheerful kisses to their wives (they did *not* go in tearfully) poised to drive away in the family car. I wonder if, in the records of history, any sane man, of his own free will, ever walked, nay argued his way, into prison!

The Hitch-Hiker

A certain policeman, said another account in the comedy of errors, was too zealous to return to work after the war. So, at his own request (there being scarce public transport by then), he was allowed to board a bus carrying prisoners from upcountry under Tanzanian escort. At every military garrison in the towns they passed by on their itinerary to Kampala, they stopped to take on board more prisoners and to send a report to their headquarters in Kampala about their journey's progress and the details of their busload using classified signals.

When they arrived in Kampala, the policeman pleaded to be allowed to go on his way but they would not let him. His departure would have caused a discrepancy in the number of prisoners they had already reported to their headquarters, and by sheer accident or carelessness the hapless cop had been counted in. Apparently the Tanzanians had a fetish about meticulous procedure and routine that by irony (if mistakenly) brought even the innocent hitch-hiker to prison!

Others had landed in prison by sheer accident or mischance. Even certified lunatics were nabbed and sent to prison. At the fall of Kampala, the inmates of Butabika, a mental asylum a few miles outside the capital, had been abandoned to their own devices. Some of them, as a result, must have strayed out of their colony and were seen wandering aimlessly by Tanzanian soldiers. Ill-dressed, dirty and shabby as they were, they might have been mistaken for Amin's soldiers stranded or affecting such a posture as a ruse to dodge capture.

Colonel Enguli

A man happened to be boozing in one of Kampala's shanty towns on one of those days when the banana leaves (paraded in ceremonial welcome of the liberating army) had not yet wilted. Even the hue and cry on Amin's soldiers had not yet lost its fervour. As was this man's habit, he became exceedingly drunk and, as a drunkard is apt to do, not only began thinking aloud but shouting out as he staggered along: "I am Colonel Enguli". This he proclaimed repeatedly with a bragging air.

Some officious Tanzanian soldiers (who happened to be there for the humble pleasures of slum life) thought that he had to be one of Amin's specimens still at large. So they arrested and sent him to Upper Prison. Far from being a colonel, the man had never seen military service in his life! The self-appointed colonel had jestingly adopted the brand of his favourite, unlicensed, grain liquor.

Lugard's Soldier

At the decree of the new Government for Amin's soldiers to report back to the army, some deserters from Amin's regime decided to do so. Even superannuated ex-servicemen—some of them with various infirmities of old age—nevertheless were enticed to return to the service, more in the belief that there was still "gold in them thar hills" than from any other motivation. What did these deadwoods get but a two-year stretch in prison instead! It was not likely by design, but due to the Tanzanians' inability to discriminate between the categories of Uganda's disbanded army, even though they pleaded to be spared for their total innocence.

The Octogenarian
The oldest inmate in the extensive range of ages at Upper Prison was a doddery octogenarian. The other inmates dubbed him *Mzekobe* (Tortoise). He was short, stooped, grey-headed (except for the bald pate), intensely wrinkled, hard of hearing, probably sand blind, had no front teeth and was too feeble even to queue for his food. He always reminded the food distributor to select the most tender piece of meat for his weak jaws and remnant bicuspids to grind, or else he would risk choking.

He recounted to a group of us in conversation that he had come from Tanzania to Uganda in his teens, before even imperial civilisation had taken root in our land. He had enlisted in Captain Lugard's regiment of Nubian mercenaries. In time he had been integrated and assimilated into the Nubian community in Bombo, where he had lived to the day of his arrest among, so to speak, latter-day gypsies from Sudan.

Asked why he was arrested, he bared his awful ebony gums as he laughed.

"Hee-hee-hee!... You know, in this world, if you have only one cow, they arrest you. If you have only one shilling, they still put you in," he said lamely.

But later I found out by chance that he had been turned in to the Tanzanians as one of Amin's Soldiers by his spiteful neighbours, who had seen him in combat fatigues in the final days of the war. Amin had sent out a desperate, swansong appeal to all ex-soldiers, even those dismissed for bad discipline, to come back and fight the war. This army fossil had gone in answer, to the Bombo Regiment near his home. He was promptly re-enlisted. Imagine how desperate Amin must have been!

In spite of his senility, the Tanzanians took him along nevertheless, possibly for his own protection rather than the accusation against him. They had also humoured his irrational accusers by doing so.

Miscellany
Incidentally, too, there was a big drove of ordinary Nubians, including juveniles, who had to seek refuge in police and prison custody because of mob threats to retaliate against them: for, generally speaking, Nubians were

known, or at least perceived to have been, Amin's most fanatical supporters and sympathisers.

Still also, the Government, for no known cause, stretched out its tentacles to some high-ranking bureaucrats of Amin's regime and to a small elite of well-known business tycoons of Kampala, or those who were deemed, undeservingly, to have the world as their oyster. This included a local motor-tyre magnate; a good-humoured, outgoing spendthrift who, as it may be recalled, was once the talk of the town during the inglorious era of "*Mafuta Mingi*" (loosely translated meaning "Fat Cat Businessmen") during Amin's hare-brained, so-called, economic war. Most of them were arrested at home or at their place of business, and a few more were arbitrarily extradited from neighbouring Kenya, where they had sought sanctuary. Similarly, military students recalled from overseas courses of training were received at the airport and delivered directly to jail.

So the net catch at Upper Prison was a promiscuous collection of, predominantly, soldiers and paramilitary members, businessmen, former ministers, ambassadors, provincial governors, district commissioners, permanent secretaries and other magnificoes right down to 14-year-old minors.

During the take, however, a young Mukiga man sustained a vicious bruise on the head. It was inflicted during the reception procedures by a vindictive warder who did not particularly like his mug, which had a strong resemblance to that of Idi Amin. The inmates facetiously renamed him Drake (pronounced, unlike the English monosyllable, without a diphthong and the accent on the second syllable), which could be as typical a name in Amin's country as is John Bull in Great Britain.

CHAPTER THREE

FLASHBACK

History is best written generations after the event, when cloud, fact and memory have all fused into what can be accepted as truth, whether it be so or not.

Theodore H White

A MERE 18-YEAR-OLD STRIPLING, I joined the army in 1968 in a voluntary enlistment almost by accident or mistake: to be honest, in the first place, I wasn't even cut out and prepared for a military career!

It seemed that the army had a custom of recruiting biennially at Eastertide. That Maundy Thursday morning, I went to the Recruitment Centre, at the Lubiri, formerly a palace of beauty and splendour, but now occupied by rude troops. It was desecrated and in the ruins following a battle that drove its former owner, Kabaka Mutesa II, into exile in a showdown with Obote in May 1966, a conflict that brought about the abolition of Uganda's four traditional (hereditary) kingdoms[1] and opened a Pandora's Box for a hitherto halcyon Uganda.

First we were taken out for a race around the extensive Lubiri wall. This road running had already disqualified a good many participants. And those who did not have any academic credentials were chased away at the double by fierce-looking, baton-wielding regimental police (RPs) at the gate, who yelled out at them a stream of abuses such as, "Run, vanish from our sight, you worthless offspring of *malayas*! You thieves of Katwe! *In iming…*"

One of them even threw his baton at the perplexed, fleeing men to show that the police were serious. Such was the treatment that they used to give to unwelcome callers.

---

1. The Kingdoms were restored in 1993 but as cultural and apolitical institutions only.

As we waited to be interviewed in turn, we observed a regimental policeman giving "a dose of discipline" to an already-initiated defaulter. He first dowsed him with a bucketful of water, then made him lie down and roll himself along the dirt before ordering him to do the frog dance, then double mark-time to the utmost limits of his stamina!

We were interviewed by a panel of brasshats, mostly, and given a medical examination by an exceedingly rude and domineering army medico, who not only barked harsh orders at us but also browbeat the *kopolo* who was assisting him at his job.

To a rookie like me, that draconian disciplinary measure, as well as the hectoring, was altogether daunting. I soon wished that I had been among the lot that had been called ignominious names and propelled away by the inhuman RPs at the gate. Perhaps it would have been better for me if I had not been recruited at all. It was to be to my sorrow that I was, for I also soon discovered that we would have to be initiated via a rigorous basic infantry course of nine months in another outback called Moroto. Then again, a rumour prevailed that our instructors would be none other than "those tough, battle-seasoned Israelis.[2] No doddle!"

As an impressionable lad who had once watched a wonderful sky-writing aerobatic show, my primary ambition — an ambition I would never after all succeed in, much to my chagrin — was to become a pilot in the Air Force (an establishment I had no idea was part and parcel of the army!). But now I would have gladly given it up so long as I was not to go for a nine-month course in Moroto, in a Godforsaken, arid region of the savage Karimojong, who were still living in pristine simplicity and backwardness, going about naked and drinking unboiled milk mixed with raw blood from their herds, ugh! So I sought the man called "Adjutant" and told him, or rather pleaded with him, that I wanted to opt out (or should I have said "chicken out"?).

He answered me in the intimidating military language that I had already been enlisted with (but oaths had not yet been administered): to leave then, I would be regarded as a deserter; so would I rather go to Luzira Prison? Timid and callow as I was, I flinched.

---

2. Actually only one Israeli Major would feature in that training to give us a one-month crash course in gymnastics for that year's colourful Independence Anniversary Tattoo at Nakivubo Stadium in Kampala.

The irony is that, had I called that adjutant's bluff, I would most probably never have gone to any prison, let alone Luzira's maximum security Upper Prison. Therefore *I would never, in the first place, have written this book—any book, in fact…!*

. . . .

ALMOST THREE YEARS LATER I had the most terrifying experience of my life. One night about four in the morning four armed soldiers mounted on a jeep were hotly pursuing me, their rifles trained on me. I ran like mad but from exhaustion, I tottered and fell down. I strained to get up but felt paralysed. If no miracle came to avert my crisis, in a few moments I would be crushed.

I was relieved, on waking-up from a nightmare, but found myself sweating and trembling. I am least inclined to believe that dreams have some bearing on happenings in real life, and, oddly enough, my nightmare could have been a premonition of the events of the following day, 25th January 1971, the day of the putsch that toppled Milton Obote.

That doomsday we set out in the morning for our daily grind as usual. But on our way to the airport we met schoolchildren trooping home; they had been turned back from school on the very opening day of the scholastic year. We became apprehensive for the first time that something was amiss.

On reaching the airport, we were at once ordered to do something until now unusual in the airforce: to load the combat planes (French-made but Israeli-modified Fouga Magisters, with bomb hatches, rocket launchers and machine guns for strafing being adapted features). We had no sooner begun loading than the hitherto quiet atmosphere was shattered by the ominous roar of a jeep-mounted 106 mm recoilless gun, and then a staccato of machine-gun fire. The International Airport terminal, only across a runway track from our base, was under siege. In an instant we were sent scooting, pell-mell, harum-scarum for the nearest cover (somewhere behind the neighbouring Uganda Aviation Company and Uganda Police Airwing hangars).

In a few minutes, the coup makers, mounted on jeeps and armoured personnel carriers (APCs), had arrived at our base too. They did not shoot anybody on sight. All of us were called, or rather coaxed, to come out of hiding, with additional persuasion from some Israeli expatriates who used to instruct and work with us (a clear indication they were privy to the coup plot and perhaps even in cahoots with the insurrectionists), and then we were mustered, purportedly for a briefing.

We were then segregated into tribal groups. The Langi and Acholi (who until then were numerically the most predominant in the army) and some others who were deemed to maintain loyalty to Obote were press-ganged into a bus and whisked away to their various dooms—most of them never to be seen again. Of course, some more unfortunate people suffered the same fate due to sheer personal grudges.

The rest of us were luckier to be spared languishing at the airport for the following three days and nights to provide watch details over it, while public reaction to the coup, especially in Buganda, was all jubilation and celebration, a wild euphoria that might have helped shroud the genocide atrocity (which, though Amin would later argue was spontaneous, could have been avoided altogether in the execution of the coup). And perhaps that was (at least partly) why even the ever-prying Western media at first glossed over the gory details of the coup, cheerily describing it only as "bloodless" and Amin himself as "a harmless gentle giant"! To the contrary, without the worldwide community knowing or suspecting, Amin had launched mass human slaughter on an unprecedented scale!

To qualify Amin as the most flagitious of contemporary dictators, a document titled "An Indictment of a Primitive Fascist Dictator" by one of anti-Amin rebel movements summed-up thus the entire nature of his barbaric reign:

> People have been choked with their genitals, their heads bashed in with sledge hammers and gun butts, hacked to pieces with pangas, disembowelled, blown up with explosives, suffocated in car boots, burnt alive in cars and houses after being tied up, drowned, dragged along roads tied to Land Rovers, starved to death, whipped to death, gradually dismembered. The luckier ones have simply been shot—and what luck is that? Even they are mutilated afterwards!
>
> Extracted from David Martin's *General Amin*.[3]

---

3. *General Amin* (1974), David Martin, Faber and Faber.

To complement my tale, I merely attempt here to chronicle Amin's 1970s only sketchily; for the more I try to write about the subject, the more I feel I am flogging a dead horse and pontificating to my betters at that! So, anyway, please excuse my rehash.

Uganda-Tanzania hostilities — to the degree of a Cold War at first — triggered-off immediately with the coming of Amin's regime. That was inevitable and least surprising because Tanzania's President Julius Nyerere (Obote's longtime mentor) utterly denounced Amin's coup while he gave sanctuary to Obote, whom he explicitly continued to regard as the President of Uganda!

The first armed conflict took place in September 1972 when a relatively small band of Ugandan exiles invaded Uganda from Tanzania (amid a hurried exodus of harried Asians, about 50,000 of whom Amin had expelled from the country, which had already earned him a chorus of international condemnation, and which also triggered-off plenty of dire shortages of basic consumer commodities in the whole country).

The invasion became just another fiasco, which the Western press, by a fitting analogy, dubbed "Nyerere's Bay of Pigs", as the ill-equipped invaders, composed of mostly Langi and Acholi tribesmen, were routed with a heavy loss of life — no quarter whatsoever was given even to those captured alive or surrendering. (But, in spite of such reverses, the Langi and Acholi could not be daunted to the extent of utter defeatism, hence Amin's unending lust for their blood).

Becoming a dead letter almost as soon as it had been signed, a peace pact hastily concluded in Mogadishu, Somalia, only saved what could at that moment have escalated into an all-out war between the two neighbours, as Cold War hostilities persisted, only a little short of a war of attrition.

Relations with Tanzania in particular (not to mention a few other countries too) continued to go from bad to worse as did Amin's unpopularity at home. Even his closest cronies continued to fall out with him, such as his own brother-in-law who, like several of his peers, deserted his ministerial job for exile! Amin, who seemed to have the proverbial nine lives of a cat, survived several assassination and coup attempts, which was cause enough for his ever-mounting fear, suspicion and unpredictability.

In February 1977, a new crisis added yet another landmark to Amin's reign of terror. After publicly accusing some people of conspiring to topple his government by force of arms, Amin ordered the arrest and (presumably) the subsequent murder of two of his own Cabinet ministers and a renowned Anglican Archbishop (in whose honour a street is now named). Amin had earlier claimed that the three were members of the cabal or a "Fifth Column" or something to that effect.

As if this prime murder of the triad was not enough cause for remorse, a holocaust was under way concerning the Langi and Acholi soldiers, allegedly the hirelings in an insurrection plot, supposedly masterminded by Obote in Tanzania.

Anyway, Amin's claim of an insurrection plot could have been at least partly true. But, for the Langi and Acholi soldiers, enough was enough! Virtually all the rest of them that had hitherto survived Amin's series of mass slaughters fled—while the fleeing was still good.

Obote's proximity in Tanzania plus the great build-up of exiles (civilians and soldiers alike) had become, so to speak, a Sword of Damocles hanging over Amin. Intelligence reports (true or false) warned him of yet another impending invasion from Tanzania. To crown it all, fresh trouble seemed to be brewing for him within the ranks of his own, kindred officers and men. So how would Amin, at his most paranoid, remedy such a state of affairs once for all? All he found was a double-edged dagger to solve both problems: for the home a diversionary ploy, and with a possible fresh Tanzanian invasion, a pre-emptive attack.

Since Amin's rise to power, his army's numerical strength had trebled (but so had their problems). Amin had "mechanised" nearly all regiments and acquired a squadron of modern, supersonic, MiG 21 jet fighters: certainly his greatest source of military hubris over Nyerere, and the cause of a grave military imbalance in the East African region and therefore of great disquiet in other neighbouring countries. More so, particularly, did Tanzania—whose army airwing was then reported by the western media to be "only patching-up the wings" of much older and retired MiG 19s—appear to be "a sitting duck".

As a matter of fact, Amin, resorting to brinkmanship of sorts, in one of his sabre-rattling public utterances, had threatened that unless Nyerere stopped harbouring and aiding his enemies, he would march into Dar es Salaam in a matter of "days", and perhaps that was his actual, megalomaniac ambition and scheme. So, one day, in one of his typical fits of bellicosity and shows of strength (Fascist style), Amin let fly with the first punch: It is widely believed (rightly or not) that he gave marching orders to one of his savage commanders, a pint-sized, jug-eared lieutenant colonel, at the head of a cracked, gung-ho regiment, complemented by MiG 21 air raids (actually at first milk-runs: with no risk whatever of confronting enemy interceptors or counter-offensive ground-to-air missiles), to steamroller and seize Tanzanian terrain with a scorched-earth policy.

Alas, even babes and sucklings, we are told, were impaled on spits like barbecues! Needless to say women were gang-raped; booty consisting of all kinds of goods and chattels was pillaged.

Tanzania's reaction to Amin's outrage of late-October 1978 was least unexpected and quite understandable. There were clarion calls to arms in this united socialist republic. The international community was no less outraged by Amin's naked aggression. Thus Amin had also played into the hands of the dissident Ugandan exiles and the Fifth Columnists: Their cause and preparedness were enhanced. In fact, never had they found so much occasion to take up arms openly against Amin!

In Moshi, a town at the foot of Mount Kilimanjaro, 20-odd loose factions convened meetings to form a unified front against Amin. Thus was created the "Uganda National Liberation Front" (UNLF). And, together with the Tanzania People's Defence Forces, they started prosecuting the war against Amin, soon after his provocation, until they dislodged his diabolical regime, all for the sake of liberation.

During and soon after the war there were all sorts of accusations and sweeping allegations that the entire Amin soldiery, as if they were a group of self-same individuals, were ill-disciplined, murderous free-booters, and hence the pretext for "preventive detention" of them to a man and why hardly anyone cared a damn to voice any concern over their plight. Such a sweeping generalisation, or the assumption of collective guilt, or guilt by association, or whatever it is, is quite unfair, and the following episode, I hope, will serve to support my contention (without me trying to be an apologist of the Amin era whatsoever).

From the onset of the war we happened to be manning the fledgling airbase in Nakasongola. We had our specialist duties to carry out on a newly-installed instrument landing system (which included precision approach radar, among other air navigational aids) as well as providing a perimeter guard on our own. Our strength, in all, was about 300, all of us "kiwis", including an infantry detachment from neighbouring Masindi Artillery Regiment, which was manning anti-aircraft installations.

Armed with the least sophisticated weaponry and, moreover, subject to a minimum alert, we could have been easy prey, even for light enemy assault. And, as far as we were concerned, that gruelling spell of war was all beer and skittles: Let me confess (with little shame, though) that every free moment we could find after our daily grind was spent in the wildest and most carefree carousal on crude *waragi* brewed and sold to us by our camp followers at the fringes of our base confines. (Talk of playing the fiddle while Rome burns!) Hardly, therefore, did we feel the scourge of the relentless advance of the Tanzanians and their UNLA allies, and the resounding defeat that was staring us in the face, so remote were we from the theatre of war.

Our contribution to the war effort was a desperate bid to ferret out guerrillas suspected of being harboured in the neighbourhoods. Even at that stage of the war, law and order in the army was still enforced and kept as tenaciously as ever. So our express orders were: to leave and come back with no money and property of any other kind except our guns and water bottles; no undue harassment except arrest if deemed necessary; after the operation everyone would have to be searched — even to the extent of stripping to the skin if one was suspected of having looted anything; a heavy penalty awaited any violator of this code of conduct, we were deterred further.

In the small hours we set off on the mission in several contingents under good, responsible leaders. Military discipline can best be tested when the normal order has broken down: We were in a hopeless war situation here, yet we carried out the cordon-and-search operation without any mistreatment, sexual molestation, let alone killing. Nobody was deprived of any money or any other kind of property. There were a few arrests, though, of certain people for irregularities on their identity papers or for possessing none at all. But they were all released later the same day with the help of their local chiefs, who vouched for them as *bona fide* locals. There were no guerrillas, or so we thought, but evidently feelings of animosity against us were at their highest. Nobody could appreciate our leniency in the circumstances, but the point I want to make is that we had at least proved to be "good losers".

About a fortnight before the fall of Kampala to the liberating forces, we too had read the handwriting upon the wall: Amin's days were numbered. Therefore and at last, we decided to take a bus home to wait out the rest of the war.

Amin's Soldiers

CHAPTER FOUR

SALAD DAYS

My salad days
When I was green in judgement,
Cold in blood.

William Shakespeare, *Antony and Cleopatra*, Act 1, scene 5

LUZIRA IS SYNONYMOUS WITH prison, and some Ugandans (at least some of those who have once been "guests" there) might have coined proverbial sayings about it, such as the common allusion to it as a "university", probably because of the salutary effect of the jail experience. So, if you've ever sojourned in this premier slammer, you had just as well include this in your CV. From common knowledge, Luzira is a suburb about six miles south-east of Kampala, on the shores of Lake Victoria.

Luzira Prison, situated on a rise, is a synthesis of four separate penitentiaries within easy reach of one another, namely: Upper Prison, Murchison Bay Prison, Remand Prison and Women's Prison. Within this expansive area are the jailers' quarters, playgrounds and a staff training college, all bounded by a high chain link fence with the only official access from the east. At the southern end there is no need for a fence because the hill slopes down and flattens out to an unnavigable marsh of papyrus reeds, the precursor of the lake. A prisoner intending to escape would therefore not head south. On the outer fringes of the prison are a smokestack works and the commonplace shanties to be found in any other suburbs.

Upper Prison is the maximum security prison in the country, and I hear that prisoners whose sentences exceed four years must be housed here. With their industries all within its walls and fences, they need never see the horizon till they leave the prison.

Upper Prison is a configuration of long, narrow stretches of two-storeyed white-washed buildings lying generally across the north, the east, the south and the west, all interconnected to form a quadrangle. The block situated to the south, however, is not storeyed and houses the administration offices and reception hall, in which there is the only gate of arrival and departure. There is another gate (rarely used) situated to the north, to one of the workshops in the "backyard" of the prison.

Outside, around the whole quadrangle, except a section of the north side, runs a wall of fencing, in my estimation 15 feet high, parallel, about six feet from the outer walls of the quadrangle. I hear that between those walls there is yet a further dreadful abyss, at the bottom of which are strewn bottle shards and sharp pieces of rough-hewn rock to make escape even more difficult.

To the east, outside, is annexed the Condemned Section and punishment cells, whose access is directly from the reception hall along a corridor to the right as you enter. The only communication with the main prison is through a hatch in the central kitchen, from which the inmates are served their food. There is a file of tall eucalyptus trees outside, more or less parallel to the western wall.

On the roof of the administration block there are tangles of barbed wire spread across from end-to-end to hamper escape; on the roof over the reception hall there is a watchtower. There are other watchtowers, to boot, placed immediately outside the outer wall at every angle of the quadrangle. For good measure, even closed-circuit TV (not in working order) was once part of the surveillance system. These are the obstacles to an escape from Upper Prison, granted you are not under lock and key. But if you are, they are more formidable than ever. The same barriers make Upper Prison an almost impregnable fortress to any attack or rescue from the outside.

Inside Upper Prison the quadrangle has an expanse of roughly two football fields put together. A short wall bisects it from east to west, forming two sections of the prison with a communicating gate in the middle. At the north-eastern side is a cluster of buildings, which are units for the central kitchen, the laundry and three or so large workshops, all together, secluded, with another access gate to them through the bisecting wall. There is also an auxiliary kitchen (depending on gas) in the south-west wing, designated "Escapee Section".

At the time of this episode there happened to be a fairly large boat with a canopy "docked" at Upper Prison. How was this outlandish feature added here? According to a rumour, it had been seized from coffee smugglers and impounded, presumably as an exhibit. It was lying at the fringe of the playground along the bisecting wall.

The buildings, whose walls (I hear) are made of thick, solid concrete are composed of tiny, incommodious cells, medium-sized halls and large dormitories downstairs and upstairs alike, with escape-proof doors and ventilators. The walls, inside and outside, have an aged, besmeared, whitewashed drab look. All the quarters are divided into wings with private enclaves or courtyards, with a toilet or two to each. There are also communal toilets in the basement of the East Wing block.

The hospital (or more precisely infirmary) is in the north section with a ward upstairs provided with beds and mattresses for in-patients; and there is another room downstairs for treating out-patients. Somewhere in this section too is installed a row of showers, in the open, with only a low wall as a screen. Part of the ground in the north section is bare with sand, which is dedicated for volleyball, and the rest is a cheap paving. In this section too there is a tree or two with luxuriant canopies, and there are a few neglected, nondescript plants along some of the walls of the buildings. A huge water tank sits on a lofty steel tower in the centre of this section.

The south section has an expansive green lawn, which is practically a football field, without (I suspect) standard dimensions. There are decorated steel columns propping-up the eaves over the verandah, and well tended flowers are lining up ceremonially in front of the office block. There is a rectangular projection, from the reception hall into the quad, of a chain link fence, through which one can peer into the reception hall through another middle gate of steel grating. My panorama of the locale is, of course, subject to error and omission, and its exact map is best not supplied for the sake of discreetness.

According to the time-honoured military tradition that superiors should not mix and fraternise with their subordinates lest they should breed contempt, army officers, together with their civilian peers, were separated from the rest, in two wings at the eastern side. The rank and file (I belong to this category) occupied the rest of the six wings or so. The wings in turn were divided into wards, which were occupied, generally, by about 50 inmates each, who, as a unit, would share a large tray of *ugali* and a bucket of vegetables.

·····················

IN SPITE OF THE rather harsh reception we received on entry to Upper Prison, we still found it hard to believe that we had totally lost our freedom and rights; we would not entertain any notion that we had become prisoners in the full sense of the word, for we still commonly held the view and belief that we were here merely on another brief sojourn, destined for better things.

Such was how naïve and so green as salad were we that from the very beginning of our stay in prison we even presumed to exercise the same freedom of expression that had come into vogue everywhere in the country after Amin's exit. Therefore, we still tried to assert our full human and democratic rights on account of our innocence and faultlessness. What justification was there to put us in prison, to be trampled underfoot? Presuming almost to dictate matters, the inmates demanded some moderation and flexibility of the draconian prison code, to which the indulgent commissioner inclined his ear.

The first thing the prisoners rejected was keeping them under lock and key, and they were promptly humoured. So there would be no lock up at any time of day or night. All the same, the inmates soon jammed all the locks with urine and salt or forcibly damaged them just in case this privilege was revoked.

We were free to roam all over the place and mix among ourselves as we liked. There would be neither arbitrary bedtime imposition nor early wake-up call in the morning. We were not to be bothered with head counts either, and, needless to say, there would be no compulsory labour.

So, with the suspension of the draconian regime and routine, not only the prisoners were appeased but also the warders stood to gain, as their chores were thereby reduced, which gave them opportunity to take French leave for other pursuits. And to us it also meant that from then on we were, so to speak, our own masters and our own keepers in prison.

But this leeway or departure from the rules was soon turned into flagrant abuse and insubordination, to fulfil the old adage. Some prisoners were soon taking a liberty as, among other things, they started regarding the warders as, at best, their equals. As soon as they had become acquainted and familiar with them through their petty business dealings they started despising them, bluntly; eventually they even engaged them in altercations and brawls. I was later to observe a case in point: A warder, having earlier walked out on some inmates, reappeared one dark evening after a couple of months of absence, so confident his creditors would not be able to recognise him; but he was wrong, for they did, and surrounded him to demand back there and then what he owed them. Since he could not produce their money, they wrested from him, after a tussle, a bundle of peanuts he had brought to sell. Most of them were spilled in the scramble.

The prison quartermaster had no immediate solution to our lack of bedding and the congestion that was mounting every day. The bare concrete "bed" was to remain our way of life. The few inmates who owned blankets, or even trash for bedding, were now envied. In time, however, as we became accustomed and insensitive to these hardships, we shelved the complaint. Besides, they were, in most of us, tempered by the stoicism of military lifestyles and endurance.

But the worst scourge of our anguish was mostly want of food. At first there was no proper arrangement to feed the enormous number of prisoners, particularly at Upper Prison. We found the kitchens there cold and they were to remain so for several weeks before they went into use again. In the meantime, food was always conveyed from Murchison Bay Prison by a tractor towing a trailer, a laborious and time-consuming process. It was even worse if inmates had to fetch it under their own steam whenever that conveyance was not available at all. In that case we would receive our vegetables contaminated by the carriers, who could not help taking pauses on the way to dip their dirty claws into it, as they would be so hungry and tired. And in that case too, we would receive our helpings much later in the evening than otherwise.

One Spartan fare a day seemed to be the utmost hospitality the prison could afford us and the only means on which we would subsist for the best part of our stay in prison. As it was the only meal in 24 hours, always coming at sunset or dusk, it found everybody's stomach tortured by fierce round-the-clock hunger pangs that brought out the worst in most of us. Even the gentleman officers could have stooped to the disgrace of scrambling for it!

The food was almost invariably *ugali* and beans (the "official" staple of our public institutions from time immemorial), but the quality and the taste varied widely, depending on the brand of the flour, and the skill and even the mood of the cook. The *ugali* might come half baked, so might the oft-weevil-infested beans, moreover unsalted sometimes! I need hardly say that our food always arrived when it had gone too cold to relish it, to speak nothing of the unhygienic conditions in which it had passed.

At first quite a few prisoners could not resist the temptation and urge to scramble. Those, however, who would always scruple to do so had to go without food for sometimes two or three successive days, as they could not (or would not) compete in the violent free-for-all. As a matter of fact, the chances of getting food in the scrambling match were so slender that the effort was hardly worth it; for even if you managed to grab a handful of *ugali*, the greatest difficulty was to extricate yourself from the scrum of other scramblers in full cry over the same object. The chances were that someone else in that helter-skelter would snatch your handful from you in turn.

Typically, whenever food was brought for a particular ward and laid down to be served, the queue would promptly fall in before it. One or two men would start distributing it. Only the front part of the queue would receive their portions in peace; but before long, the tail of the queue would start wagging, that is fidgeting and stirring with impatience; and someone would be trying to jump the queue for fear that the grub would be over before his turn came. If that happened, the queue would suddenly become a melee, with men stampeding for the food, with deafening cheers of "Charge … charge…" piercing the air in the process. The aftermath of the scrambling would at times leave more food sprinkled on the ground than was actually taken by the scramblers. This food, some of the scramblers who were unsuccessful would still retrieve, dust-off and, alas, proceed to eat, unabashedly!

The main cause of scrambling was undoubtedly the apparent shortage of food, which was made still worse by the inequitable distribution of it to the various wards. Some wards with fewer inmates would sometimes be allotted more food than other wards with more inmates, simply because nobody cared to organize anything. The problem was made yet worse by a breed of Oliver Twists and Artful Dodgers seeking or pinching another helping. Typically, such a person would receive his due share of food from his genuine ward in good time to shift to another queue unnoticed. In those early days of our residence in prison the wardmates did not know everyone for sure, so it would be difficult if not impossible to discriminate against outsiders, who after all would cause artificial shortages for other wards.

Food scrambling was perpetrated particularly at the northern section of the prison, which was occupied largely by the mindless and heedless youths and juniors of the army, who had a propensity for sheer hooliganism and other indiscretions of youth. For their food riots and other frequent fracases, even a *slugfest* once in a while, the northern section of the prison was aptly nicknamed "Soweto" (the once riot-prone Black township of apartheid South Africa). At the southern section of the prison, which was occupied mainly by the older and gentler folk of the army, such scrambling was not so widespread and frequent.

Try as the warders might, they could not rein in the queues to bring about an equitable and orderly distribution of food. So, some Tanzanian soldiers, confident that they would be as good as troubleshooters they ever were, decided to take charge of the queues. At first they would be toting their guns, for they seemed to have in their code a prohibition on going near "Amin's Commandos" without a gun.

But it seems the prison authorities did not approve of their rather extraordinary precaution for the reason that even an accidental gunshot inside there could easily spark off undue panic for the inmates, which could cause them to try to escape or mutiny. Therefore they had a rule which forbade carrying guns inside the prison just as long as there was no due cause to do so. Only in special circumstances of emergency might guns be wielded as the last resort. Furthermore, the prison authorities contended, the very contrary of their precaution was the safer rule: Never go near a prisoner (let alone a commando) with a gun.

Indeed, some of the Tanzanian soldiers were not infrequently drunk and seemingly careless of their guard, circumstances that could tempt some desperate prisoner to try to wrest the gun from them. But, in the first place, the prisoners themselves should have been relieved of the danger from disorderly, trigger-happy soldiers that some of those Tanzanians were apt to be. So, anyway, the Tanzanians were apparently prevailed upon by the caution of the prison officers; instead they resorted to their swagger sticks, with which they still used strong-arm tactics to control the queues. But before long they also gave that up, having accomplished nothing.

Then a certain man, no more than an inmate himself (I shall call him The Chieftain), asserted his authority to save us this chaos, to the welcome, though, of the prison keepers and the inmates themselves. A venerable colleague no less senior than Amin in the service, The Chieftain also rose from the humble ranks to the rank of colonel. He was well-known and respected not only in the army but also in household circles for his long illustrious career as the parade marshal of the Uganda Army. Some people would refer to him in dramatic style as "Professor of Parade". Amin last appointed him commandant and caretaker of the swanky edifice of the General Army Headquarters in Kampala.

A six footer, The Chieftain, who might also deserve a knighthood, would somewhat resemble Sir Winston Churchill, were it not for the sharp contrast in skin colour, The Chieftain's being jet black. He used to joke in bad English, for, alas, in his prime he received no more than the benefit of the rudimentary three r's, his lack of higher schooling being his only shortcoming for the role of one of the finest officers and gentlemen. Yet I often saw him carrying an English novel! And I once heard The Chieftain, who has a dialectical handicap with sibilants, say that his age was "fifty-chicks."

Remarkably too, he was a phenomenon of long British military upbringing, brainwashing and bigotry. Unlike most of his peers, however, he affected the simplest taste in dress and displayed none of that elitist arrogance and snobbery, never losing the common touch with the lower ranks. (A man of the people, you might say.) But, to complete his profile, a sterner martinet than The Chieftain never lived! Such was his reputation and charisma that he commanded respect and was able to wield control over the forlorn soldiers.

The Chieftain was thus given a free hand to marshal our stay and destiny at Upper Prison. So he at once set about the task of abolishing food scrambling, which became popularly known by the military jargon "charging". He first appointed certain judicious officers, including a member of the bar (I shall designate them the Brains Trust), who would now and then advise him on the manifold problems concerning our stay and welfare, and constitute a sort of kangaroo court to settle our in-house disputes.

I have earlier lamented that what we lacked in the first place was systematic organization and self-control—a form of self-government, as it were, among prisoners—to effect a fair distribution of the food. The Chieftain and his Cabinet of wise men came up with the first obvious solution: The genuine roll call of every ward had to be ascertained. Each ward had to appoint, democratically, a ward leader and an assistant to have charge over them. Those elected as leaders would have to ensure a fair distribution of food to their ward mates. They would also be responsible for the upkeep of discipline, a breach of which they might report to The Chieftain to take measures if need be. Any matter outside The Chieftain's purview or discretion could be taken up with the Prison Superintendent, to whom he would always have prompt access.

So far so good. The distribution of food from the kitchen to the various wards could be adjusted equitably. To avoid the inconveniences of ferrying food from Murchison Bay, a temporary kitchen was soon erected. When this makeshift kitchen was ready with piles of firewood, cooking vessels and other related things, The Chieftain himself appointed former cooks in the army to staff it. And when it came into full use, shortages and scrambling ceased: firstly because our kitchen was always able to cater for more than what used to be allotted from Murchison Bay Prison; secondly because there would always be provident food, too, set aside in case of an unforeseeable shortage or discrepancy such as might be caused by newly arrived prisoners or lodgers (prisoners in transit to other destinations); and thirdly because the ward leaders themselves employed a meticulous method to distribute the food by relying on the roll call to preclude any repeater or intruder. Everyone was therefore assured of getting his rightful share in peace. Each ward leader would, of course, be entitled to a sovereign's share of the rations as his perk and motivation.

It was not long before the auxiliary kitchen was also supplied with gas, and The Chieftain recruited more cooks to operate it. Their stint would be to cook food for about one hundred "special diet" beneficiaries, whose food consisted of only occasional supplies of rice and Irish potatoes, but otherwise they also depended largely on the ordinary diet. From this kitchen also, lunches would be allotted to bedridden patients, to invalids and to the feeble, senile men like Lugard's soldier, alias Mzekobe.

Thus The Chieftain had overcome our worst scourge, but that is not to say his mandate never met with opposition: One day as a lorry was delivering to the kitchen, some inmates invaded it and started grabbing potatoes, although the off-loaders tried hard to balk them. As chance would have it, however, The Chieftain himself materialised to catch the looters red-handed! He rebuked them in anger and ordered them to put the potatoes back and "Clear out." Some of them obeyed, whilst others artfully made away with some of their booty, and one of them stuck to his guns. Clinging to his potatoes, he confronted The Chieftain with stubborn impertinence:

"Who anointed you head over us?... Remember, in prison we are all level", he said as he crunched on one of them... How do you expect me to take orders from a fellow prisoner like you?"

The old man, with a lump in his throat at such a rebellious affront, found no words to confront him, and he simply ignored the villain with resignation.

The Chieftain could, of course, have had this rebel arraigned before the superintendent for correction, which, in all probability, would have been corporal punishment, but this he was probably averse to. So the matter was condoned.

The Brains Trust, however, found a solution to keep away these human vultures from the kitchen during the busy hours. A number of inmates were appointed and designated as "kitchen police", whose mission would be to guard the kitchen daily and to ensure that no unauthorised person gained access or came near it, and they might, if they found it necessary, use brute force. Happily for them, they would be eating as much as the cooks themselves. So, when they zealously took up their duty and post, armed with bludgeons and showing the physiques of warriors or prizefighters (the choosers really knew what's what), nobody for some time afterward, without a good excuse, ever haunted our kitchen again. Once more our own troubleshooters had triumphed.

• • • • • • • • • • • • • • • • • • •

AT THE SAME TIME that Upper Prison was being populated it was also being stocked with looted articles for their safe custody. The wanton and widespread ransacking at the fall of Kampala to the liberating forces had spared nothing in shops, factories, hotels, garages, residences, schools and offices—not even stretchers and trolleys from hospitals. I learnt they were used for carting away heavy loot!

The new Government had subsequently decreed that all looted goods be restored to their owners; and, as a result, the looters had only partly responded by returning and abandoning some of the goods that they did not find much use for, leaving them by the roads and streets, which had soon become littered with innumerable articles of all kinds. Lorry-loads of these items were gathered up and dumped in the prison workshops. There were chairs of every kind, tables, desks, benches, fridges and cookers stripped of their vital components, motor-bikes devoid of their engines and wheels; filing cabinets, and so on. I doubt if any of these things ever found their way back to their owners at all.

The inmates in turn invaded the workshops and helped themselves to these spoils at one fell swoop, leaving only those that were too heavy to be carried about or that were without any use at all. Incidentally, they also looted from the workshops such things as sisal, tanned hides and skins, aluminium sheets, various kinds of craftsmen's tools and many other oddments.

The inmates appropriated for themselves the cosiest sofas, swivel chairs, wicker basket chairs, dining chairs, office chairs and other kinds of seating, which they would use mostly for basking in the sun. Some of them who owned rocking and revolving chairs would rock and spin round in them and really enjoy their recreation. Another on such a chair would be given a "rolling stroll" on castors, in idle sport. (The luckiest inmate was the one who owned a dentist's chair!) And what's more, some of them, lounging thus on their chairs, claimed homage and were made to feel and affect the attitude of big wheels by some obsequious warders who usually came to them stomping their boots: clump, clump, thud-thud, freezing at attention, fawning on them, "*Afende…*" One of them was even said to give the stiff hand salute with abandon to one such prisoner!

Such were the actions of the warders, plying errands between the prisoners and their families and they were sometimes rewarded for a single errand more than their month's salary, say, if a delivery of 10,000 shillings (a princely sum in those days) was made from a family or bank. (A prison warder's monthly salary then was a paltry 600 shillings). But among them there were also some fly-by-night conmen who eventually walked out on their partners with relatively big sums of money and kept out of sight thereafter.

·····················

Kampala's southern inner city of Katwe has for long borne abuse as a byword for places of ill-fame, or the underworld. (Any wonder, then, that the police have kept an outpost there?) To this name-calling is a more recent addition of ridiculous, yet curious coinage, "Radio Katwe", meaning "rumour mill"! Although the name is derisory, it proved to be a more reliable news source than the state-controlled Radio Uganda of Amin's day. During the war people cynically came to regard Radio Uganda as the rumour-monger (for which read "lie-monger"). In prison, especially, we perhaps overused the term more than the household name.

From the very start of our stay in prison we were obsessed with rumours about our fate, and the inmates spent nearly all their time gadding about the place in search of or fabricating them. Although there were several radios among the inmates, few cared to listen to them for national broadcasts, which presented then mostly obloquies on Amin, Amin's henchmen, Amin's thugs and Amin's what have you. Even fewer concerned themselves with the adverse publicity appearing in the various newspaper columns.

No sooner had we settled in prison than we started entertaining hopes and illusions of leaving it — the following day or the following week. We were fed with rumours which we ourselves were so keen not only to listen to but to take as true, and bandy them about. Such rumours made us happy and full of hope in spite of the hardships and dire want we were living in. Our hardships were indeed tempered by our great expectations to be quit of them soon and back to fleece the taxpayers again. We even shelved our complaint for the right to sleep between blankets, more food and other amenities. To sum it up figuratively, the rumours and the illusions about our imminent release were the opium — the very antidote — to our hardships and woes. So, if a man felt homesick too, he would seek such rumours to find solace in; but even if there was no fresh rumour come lately to allay his homesickness, the rumour dispensers might still find him some sort of placebo instead. Suffice it to say, if you banished rumours from us, you would have robbed us of our fools' paradise.

One of the first events that Radio Katwe predicted correctly, without even the superintendent's formal announcement, was the coming of the Red Cross *Bazungu* to our aid. Indeed they came after a week or two of our stay in prison, empty-handed except for some portfolios under their arms, to note down our problems. They were accompanied by a tall, broad-shouldered, bull-necked officer, whom we recognised as the ADC who had helped lure us into prison from our sojourn in Makindye. A rather hulking figure of a man, he conducted the *Bazungu* on a tour around the prison while some inmates who happened to be sun-lazing at the time looked on with all manner of curiosity and attentiveness. At one point this prison officer was telling the three or so *Bazungu* without any scruples whatsoever:

"We give them three blankets each … We withdraw them in the day lest they should get lost…"

What an arrant liar! The inmates who heard him were taken over by apoplectic rage. They sprang to their feet and thronged the *Bazungu* and their lying guide.

"But, excuse me, Sirs," one of the rude ones accosted the *Bazungu*, "this man is a filthy, malicious liar." Indeed, the words were spat with a massive dose of venom.

"If there are any blankets, let him show them now", he was challenged, "he can't get away with such a bare-faced lie."

The prisoners gathered around were no less infuriated: seething, looking daggers-drawn at the prison officer. Unable to answer the challenge and withstand the brickbats of their fury, the officer marched away in utter disgrace. And even as he did so, another fusillade of invective was discharged upon him in an unbridled outburst:

"He was one of Amin's hangmen," charged one.

"Ay, that's why Amin promoted him," supplemented another.

"You traitor!"

"You turncoat!"

"You self-seeker!"

"You…"

"Okay, okay, that will do," intervened one of the continentals, and they piped down respectfully.

Then, as they were left on their own with the visitors, they began explaining in their own way and they conducted them around the wards, mentioning all of our hardships and dire needs. As a sample of our many plagues, they showed them hundreds of very fat lice (no hyperbole) which they had earlier picked and wrapped up in an envelope in readiness for their coming, thus emphasising the presence of these insects in plague-like numbers and ferocity. By the end of the tour the talks were more fruitful than would have been otherwise with the lying officer: blankets and sprays against lice were included in the relief supplies on our wish list. Then those contented inmates escorted the *Bazungu* to the gate for a friendly leave-taking.

In about the third week of our stay at Luzira the Chief-of-Staff of the Uganda National Liberation Army also came to see us in the forenoon, although we had received no prior notification even by our freelance sources. He took us quite by surprise and there was even second-guessing, as we trooped to the assembly area to be addressed by him, that such an abrupt visit might terminate our stay in prison, for military orders could be so sudden and capricious. So we soon gathered ourselves before him, nearly everybody's bottom on a looted chair!

In a laconic style peculiar to generals or commanders, the Chief-of-Staff declared, "You are not imprisoned; you are merely confined."

"Confined" is more mitigating, or the lesser of two evils, we all seemed to understand this, so, naturally, we expressed our approval by clapping our hands. He went on:

"Any country is always justified to have an army at any given time under whatever leader. That is to say, despite Amin's criminal leadership, you were all pursuing a legitimate career nonetheless."

That also received a spontaneous all round applause.

Then he stated further that we would stay in prison for only a short while in order to allow them time and chance to sort out certain things first. We would leave prison "soon", he promised. The meeting ended on that note and with another round of applause.

If there were any lines to read between in that speech, I suppose none of us could do so at the time because that was at least what we had expected and wanted him to say. We could not think of anything else to the contrary; so any doubts and misgivings that might have existed were dismissed completely. We trusted his promise to the hilt; we took our "imminent departure" for granted—indeed as an act of faith.

Our rumours, and hopes for freedom, would be based on the chief's assurance with the emphatic "soon." The evenings, after glutting ourselves on *ugali*, were the best times for comparing notes. The inmates would discuss nothing else but their notions about the future army—even entertaining fatuous hopes for promotions and appointments in the new establishment; we really were in Cloud-Cuckoo-Land!

One evening while waiting for food, I overheard an elderly and corpulent sergeant-major (who was fond of sporting a rather roguish but amusing "ten gallon" hat) regaling some callow youths with his notions in a fatherly manner.

"You young lads," he said, "you need have nothing to worry about. The new regime means no harm to us, and we shall soon be absorbed into the new army. We now have better prospects than ever before. We are lucky that we were not Amin's victims, otherwise he would by now have dispatched us all to the next world—including even *you* who have not yet even tasted the sweetness of a woman."

Indeed the boys, in spite of the intense hunger, were tickled to hearty laughter at the ribald punchline.

Our next visitor was accurately predicted by Radio Katwe the day before his arrival. This was the Minister of Internal Affairs. We were assembled before him in the hot afternoon sun, and he said,

> As you should already have heard from the president himself, we did not come to even the score. Our mission was to liberate all *wananchi* from the regime of terror and murder. Just ask yourself: "If Amin had survived this war again, how many more Ugandans, including even *you*, would have been plunged into yet more bloodbaths?"

Then, with legal undertones, he said we would have to pass through a screening exercise because there was a public outcry and a terrible public grievance against a good many of us; that whereas the Government harboured no vindictive intentions for us, our own confinement in prison was the only sure way to insulate us from the potential danger posed by elements of the public, and by the same expedient the public were also protected from us, "dangerous as you are". (No doubt some of Amin's soldiers who had to dodge the lawless perils of lynch mobs must have benefited from being in the security of prison custody.) This holier-than-thou functionary concluded, "Those who will be found innocent will leave prison soon; those with specific charges against them shall answer in the courts of law." He might as well have said we were all presumed guilty until proven innocent.

He had said more or less what the previous speaker had done, except for the screening and the legal bit, a little inconsistency we could brush aside; for if you knew you were not at fault at all, what other cause was there to keep you in prison? So the rumours about our not-far-away departure continued to abound. Our Fools' Paradise was never lost.

Our fourth visitor came in the fourth week or so of our stay in prison. He also arrived unheralded even by our unofficial sources. It was the Minister of Defence who stood before us in the morning, and reiterated his colleague's point but added sourly, "You were the tools of a murderous reign! You are now going through the dip to purge you of your ticks. Each of you must be screened singly…" At the end of his diatribe he did not want to hear any questions, but perhaps out of respect for our protagonist, The Chieftain only was allowed to air his pent-up plea.

The Chieftain snapped to respectful attention and, standing stock still, spoke more or less thus:

> Sir, when our country was freed from the clutches of the dictator Idi Amin, we were no less happy than other citizens; when the new Government recalled the remnant soldiers, we came obediently, without fear or misgivings, confident that we have never committed any crimes. You know, Sir, our position is the same as that of a widow, who must by custom be inherited by another husband. That is why we are here gathered all true sons of Uganda, pledging to you our full support and readiness to assist the new Government in its hard challenge of rebuilding our dear country from the present ruins. Now that Amin and of his ilk have gone, let us return to the old spirit of brotherly love and unity without fear or suspicion.

The audience applauded The Chieftain's speech but the Minister spurned the overture, saying that the words he had already spoken were still his answer. Then The Chieftain pleaded that we be allowed to see our families.

The minister was as adamant as ever: "In all my eight years of exile I never saw my father and mother. Now, do you want us to bring your families to stay with you in prison?..." Soon afterwards, the meeting broke up dispiritedly.

Although the Defence Minister's speech had been disheartening, carrying no equivocation whatever, most prisoners would nevertheless still doubt his seriousness about screening each individual one of us, our number being in several thousands. How could this be consistent with the earlier assurance that we would leave prison soon? How soon was their "soon"? A week? A month? A year? How long could they take to screen the whole lot of us? Curiouser and curiouser!

That should have been our new homework, but our starry-eyed optimists and escapists assured us there was no need to bother with computation; instead they guessed at another wild theory that the minister could not reveal their true intentions yet, as they might have found it necessary to hoodwink a few people whom they had predestined to keep in prison. Even such opinion was generally accepted or wished to be true.

Seeking further assurance, some superstitious prisoners also consulted self-styled oracles or fortune-tellers, who usually tossed a pair of sandals for dice, pretending to mumble some abracadabra, and deciphered the signs as favourable. Night dreams were also interpreted as anything but bad omens: Our departure was imminent, our "Josephs" corroborated. Even later on, another "auspice of good luck" was received from a flight of birds chirping happily as one day they made a fly-past over our prison. Certainty was made doubly certain. Our Fools' Paradise continued to thrive.

· · · · · · · · · · · · · · · · · · ·

THE PRISON AUTHORITIES SEEMED not to be troubled by our congestion, which was becoming increasingly alarming, as they continued to take more and more prisoners, much to our resentment. Although, after about a month, the massive intakes had dwindled to an average of about five new prisoners per day, one would wonder where and when they would draw the line.

They had opened makeshift wards, which were formerly stores and a laundry. These had also taken in even more prisoners, well beyond their capacity. With no more stores and laundries, it became difficult to accommodate newcomers. Warders were turned away everywhere they went in search of accommodation for even one or two prisoners who had just arrived, unless they sought the intercession of The Chieftain, to whom the inmates were more obliging. But whenever a large batch of civilian prisoners arrived, it was almost impossible, even with The Chieftain's help, to find room for them among soldiers who knew them not.

For obvious reasons, newly arrived soldiers were always able to find room easily and readily among their friends and colleagues with whom they could live in harmony. The superintendent had realised this, so one afternoon, he himself assembled the inmates of a certain ward at the Escapee Section and told them that he had heard of their discipline as the best in the prison, and as a reward he was going to transfer them all elsewhere with far better amenities than were available at Upper Prison; that their ward was going to be occupied by the most dangerous and most wanted criminals, who would have to be kept under lock and key at all times; that if anyone of them tarried there, he would find himself in the same lot with that unfortunate group; therefore they could pack up at once and wait for transport to their new destination.

It was no sooner said than done. Those inmates at once started scurrying to their ward to retrieve their belongings; and no sooner had they vacated it than a drove of about forty civilians were ushered in to occupy their places. But afterwards, the 50 or so displaced prisoners never shifted anywhere outside Upper Prison. The transport did not come that day and would never come afterward. It wasn't until about sunset of that day until it dawned on these displaced prisoners that they had thus simply become — for want of a better expression — victims of musical chairs! So they started seeking and found new lodgings among their army colleagues and friends in various other wards, where they were readily welcomed.

The superintendent had cunningly achieved his aim. He had tricked those inmates into vacating their ward for the new drove of civilians he could not have found room for otherwise. As it turned out, those civilians were not "the most dangerous and most wanted criminals, to be kept under lock and key." He was the third most inveterate liar in the prison service. After that episode he had no more cards up his sleeve to conjure-up more accommodation with or to solve the congestion problem. New prisoners, civilians in the main, who filtered in daily, were unable to find accommodation within four walls, so they took up residence on the spacious veranda of the administration building, braving the night elements. Among them was Colonel Enguli, who was not welcome in any circles, dirty and shabby as he always looked.

One of the problems that obtained in this massive concentration was the shortage of lavatories. The open-air showers, however, were never congested because one could always postpone a shower. (And this, by the way, was a fortunate thing also for those who, as a moral rule or taboo, may not look upon the nakedness of those they feared and respected, namely fathers, uncles — real or otherwise — and in-laws.)

But when one wants to defecate, one can hardly put off the act for long. The toilets, most of which were in bad shape, being clogged and their walls besmeared with excrement, even absurd graffiti such as "Kill and Pray" (probably an intended pun for "prey"), were too few for our great number, which by now was more than 2,000. One wing, for instance, had but two toilets for about 150 inmates. I note (although this may not be pertinent to congestion) that prisons do not respect the right to individual privacy, as, for example, in the case of the communal showers in the open. But there was still more to our lavatories than meets the eye. In the basement of the East Wing block there happened to be an aggregate of about 20 toilets, all within one long, narrow, unpartitioned chamber. In this dungeon, squatting-type water closets had been installed in two rows of ten each along its length, with a narrow passageway between them. With this type of convenience many prisoners could relieve themselves simultaneously, whether in large concentration or under lock and key restraint. In the latter case, particularly, a warder would have to carry out the unenviable chore of escorting a procession of a score or so of prisoners to the toilets. The prisoners parade on them in full sight of one another while the warder waits. When they have all finished their motions, he marches them back to their ward and lets out another procession, which is all in a day's work for a prison warder!

Those toilets, moreover, were always dirty and neglected, so all the more reason why most prisoners had a repugnance for this type of convenience.

But, of course, some soldiers who must have experienced similar conditions of bivouacs would not feel abashed or shy to share such intimacy. Similarly, some other wings also had double or triple latrines in one chamber without partitioning. In such congestion as ours, then, there was hardly any place where you could be at any time all by yourself—hardly even in a *choo*!

However, whenever a man wanted to urinate when he was, say, out lazing on the lawn, he did not have to run back to the toilets of the ward, which he might after all find engaged; instead he simply faced a wall and peed on it. Soon we all took up this habit and it was not long before Upper Prison started stinking to the skies of stale urine; and with the deluge of decaying, rain-soaked, maggot-ridden refuse from the kitchen, the prison looked and smelled for all the world like a dunghill or pigsty.

The superintendent became duly alarmed, so he ordered a urinal to be erected at once. Some public works men came and made a hasty construction of a urinal with running water, out against the wall curtain of the two sections of the prison. This time, however, they warded-off this facility from the side view with tin sheets in due consideration, I presume, of the beautiful svelte sister who used a route close by on her way to and from the hospital. A garbage truck was also hired for the first time to dispose of the enormous accumulation of two months' refuse.

After the first two months or so, congestion was at its peak and it seemed that Upper Prison had stopped "restocking" for a while. Our Fools' Paradise was also at its peak. Radio Katwe still maintained that our departure would come soon and abruptly like a bolt from the blue. Early one Monday morning, a sudden call assembled us before the clerks' office. According to the previous day's rumours, most prisoners believed this had to do with our exit, as a clerk appeared before us with lists of prisoners' names. He read out the names and the owners answered to them pronto, somewhat excitedly. About 150 of us were called thus and afterwards told to pack up for a journey to up-country jails. This was to be just the first of several false dawns we were to experience about our release.

During the rest of that week more prisoners were posted up-country, and eventually a total of about 600 privates and junior ranks were drained out of Upper Prison to ease congestion. Here we at first gave up hope and our spirits flagged. Our rumours were stifled but not for long. Our Fools' Paradise seemed to succumb to a cheerless suspense.

·····················

THE EARLY DAYS SAW off out of the prison the sacrosanct chaplains, presumably by special request and pressure from the Catholic hierarchy because they were short of pastors to herd the flock at large. That left us deprived of our priests for the daily services and *shriving*. Along with them were seen off several other persons too. How they were singled out is anybody's guess.

On two occasions the Minister of Internal Affairs (who earlier spoke to us) was seen with the commissioner in the dark evening hours touring the prison and affecting to taste the prisoners' food! On each occasion they prowled about until an unseasonable hour. Their aim, rumour claimed later, was to release secretly certain relations and friends of theirs.

Rumour also had it that a good number of prisoners absconded on various nights via the gate by greasing the palms of the turnkeys. That was not improbable either, with most of our venal keepers so much wanting for means to cope with runaway inflation. As the customary procedures and routine of the prison were disrupted, with no daily head counts, for one thing, the higher prison authorities could never come to find out anything. The warders started doing a count of the prisoners — on waking up in the mornings only — only much later on, not even by physical enumeration but by merely copying the figures from the ward leaders, who invariably proclaimed the number from their muster rolls.

A group of daredevils effected their escape by scaling and abseiling down the wall during one pitch-dark night. The act was disguised and obscured in a noisy uproar of merrymaking with drumming and folk-dancing all night long, creating an effective diversion. The drums were improvised with old, disused buckets (acquired from the kitchens) and for drumheads they used animal skin (misappropriated from the prison workshops). By analogy, here was yet another episode of "The Wooden Horse". The drums would represent the vaulting crate: the drumming, the folk-dancing and the noisy play around it all helped create optimum circumstances for some inmates to escape — over the fence. The graveyard shift sentry, even if he was posted to observe his beat, could easily be distracted from his vigilance, confident there was really nothing to worry about in a merrymaking, devil-may-care, happy-go-lucky bunch of prisoners; falling for the trick, he could even go to slumber. Moreover, the evidence of the escape was provided by ropes seen the next morning dangling somewhere on the northern wall at Soweto, where the nightlong revelry was staged. Strange though this may seem, the authorities never made a fuss over the matter. How many escaped in that manner is anybody's guess.

A certain inmate also escaped in broad daylight by boarding a lorry that had just delivered potatoes to the kitchen, thus sneaking out as a member of the lorry's crew. But a young medical officer was graciously granted leave to attend his father's funeral. Although he could have stayed away, he did come back! Later on, another officer also sought compassionate leave, but the authorities had by now become wary, so they told him to stay put.

· · · · · · · · · · · · · · · · · · ·

THE EARLY DAYS ALSO ushered in all manner of commercial enterprise in the prison. The first stock in trade was cigarettes smuggled in by prison warders and the Tanzanian guards, and peddled by inmates, who sold them to fellow inmates, furtively at first. It was not long before business started gaining momentum, and soon nearly everybody, especially the youngsters of Soweto, was involved in one kind of business or another. The youngsters made business leagues with the warders and the Tanzanian guards, and it was not long before a spate of articles other than cigarettes also found their way in: soap, sugar, salt, canned foods, various kinds of pastries and candies, peanuts, stationery, over the counter drugs — the catalogue is endless. Eventually even *enguli* was introduced into the traffic.

The commodities were smuggled in daily and mostly at the remotest and darkest hour of night. Through their trade pursuits, our youths befriended, familiarised and established strong associations with the warders and the Tanzanian guards. All the prison turnkeys were in collusion with their Tanzanian co-keepers to allow the contraband into the prison, and the superintendent apparently connived at their conspiracy presumably on humanitarian grounds for the prisoners, whom he could not otherwise provide with such basic essentials. At least those who had money could get what they wanted.

Perhaps the greatest bootlegger of them all was the portly 50-year-old executioner, who was not carrying out any executions at the time, presumably because the death chamber was also under rehabilitation. He had the monopoly (whether by arrangement or not) to supply the native gin, and his hour of delivery (by arrangement with his consignee) was at the signal of first cock-a-doodle-doo and a loud bow-wow, which always announced his approach. At these signals his consignee (who must have been a light sleeper) would wake up and go out to the gate to collect a jerry can or two of the potent distillate. The 40 litres or so of *enguli* would be distributed to several retailers. The retailers in turn would dispense it in the privacy of their cells during the daytime, but at night they had no need to fear exposing it in the illumination of the outside lamps at Soweto to be consumed on the pavement.

The runaway inflation price of this liquor was hiked to about three times the price of that of the original beer barons outside the prison. Therefore, with money in short supply, only a very few prisoners were able to afford it, and hardly anyone could afford to buy more than was good for him. There are many more excuses, other than just dipsomaniac addiction, for drinking. Ours was mainly to nurse our frustrations and to induce sleep quickly. We had hardly any instances of outrageous misconduct as a result of over-drinking. So the liquor flow continued unchecked and unhindered. The warders themselves not only condoned it, but even encouraged the tippling parties: Whenever they too felt like boozing, they would simply do it in our calaboose.

Another bonanza was found in a store which was opened to about 60 inmates to ease congestion. Inside they found a pile of no fewer than 1,000 motor-tyre inner-tubes, which they spread out to sleep on. That was another instance of letting a horse sleep on hay and expect it not to chew any of it. Those fortunate inmates soon conspired with some of the warders to smuggle and sell the inner tubes outside for money which they shared. In the long run they must have filched almost half the tubes before the storeman at last discovered their racket. Well, the storeman rescued the rest by switching them over to another store in the same prison, quietly.

The other goods were soon spread out in the open under the shade of trees or in the glare of the sun, quite in the fashion of the flea markets downtown. They were laid out on tables, on stools, on benches and on cardboard boxes, which served as shop counters. The bulk of this trade was carried on at Soweto, from where issued a loud babble of voices touting wares with high pressure catchpenny advertising phrases.

In addition to that, more businesses yet were established to supplement the one-meal-a-day subsistence: tea, coffee and porridge were made and taken at any time regardless of the temperature of the day. So if a man ordered a beverage, he might also order a scone, a cake or peanuts to accompany it. The beverages were prepared in tins, pails and other kinds of pans misappropriated from the kitchen, from where firewood was also pinched for cooking. (Wood shavings from the carpentry workshop came in handy as tinder.) Thus firewood became one of the most sought-after resources at Upper Prison. Whenever there was no firewood supply from the kitchen, they tore down tree boughs and branches; and they started stripping the derelict boat of its timber by degrees. The plastic sanitary pails (humorously called prisoners' briefcases) were all soon immolated for cooking. Chairs and other kinds of wooden furniture were sacrificed in the same way. When all those resources were spent and they could find no other fuel, they searched the garbage heap for dry potato peelings and banana skin—and any other kind of junk that could come aglow for cooking; whence came this epigram: In Upper Prison all but shit's pay dirt! Thus all caution had been cast to the winds and business was now conducted out in the open in full swing, and the operators prospered in earnest endeavour and competition.

With all this happening—the merchandising and its noisy advertising, the crowds of inmates milling about to shop or drink tea, the widespread cooking raising thick puffs of smoke aloft, the clatter and clanging of men breaking wood or shaping some metal—it seemed we were on a veritable picnic.

This market scene, where gambling on card games was also carried on in earnest, was always staged at Soweto, which was a safe distance from the superintendent's office. The superintendent, however, only indirectly made it understood that, although he condoned the influx of those commodities, his *laissez faire* attitude couldn't tolerate them being spread out on display, making his prison look like a *sokoni*. So, whenever the superintendent was seen emerging from his office purporting to head thither, a timely signal would warn all the businessmen to spirit away their wares before he arrived. This was executed so adroitly and so expeditiously that you would think there had been nothing going on for hours before. Even the smoke that was hovering above only moments ago would be made to cease suddenly.

On one occasion, however, one merchant was caught with his pants down. It was on one of those days when the auxiliary kitchen happened to be in operation and the inmates were permitted to draw hot water from there in the morning to make tea or to soak their lousy clothes. It so happened that some businessmen laid out at the scene things to accompany tea. At the signal for the superintendent's approach, all of them had their goods hidden in a jiffy. But one tardy man, who was probably lost in a reverie, was cornered like a rat. Before he could recover his composure, the superintendent came up to him. Startled, he hastily covered his jar with a lid and stood up.

"What have you got there?" the superintendent demanded harshly and glaringly.

"Sir, I only came to get hot water." The lame answer could not have convinced anybody.

"All right, pour it out in the gutter," the superintendent challenged.

A silence ensued as the victim, defenceless and speechless, just stared at his assailant. Only sniggers could be heard from some of the onlooking prisoners, who seemed to derive fun from the awkward fix this poor fellow was in.

Then, unexpectedly, in the next moment, the superintendent's serious expression transformed into a gracious smile, as he walked away, to the victim's relief.

Thereupon everyone released a roar of laughter at the absurdity of losing two kilogrammes of precious sugar in the filthy, clogged-up gutter. Sugar was a boost to the prisoners' diet, and the superintendent, having caught a glimpse of the contents of the jar, surely would not have allowed such a waste even for the sake of the rules. He was merely teasing the poor fellow.

There were also some other aspects of industry that attended this commercial activity and spawned craftsmen of all sorts. In a community as large and promiscuous as ours, there abounded seamsters to patch up our torn and threadbare clothes for a fee; shoe repairers also asserted their trade and repaired broken shoes and worn-out sandals and flip-flops; they mended handbags, wallets and other leather goods. All their raw materials were purloined from the prison workshops. With the sisal therefrom, the weavers, apart from making ropes for escaping, also fashioned other innocent articles such as mats, hats, satchels, loofahs and even sackcloth.

Then there were the tinsmiths and the tinkers, who found a fair share of aluminium sheets from the said workshops and shaped crude non-standard-sized tablespoons, teaspoons and ladles; they repaired bottomless or leaking pans and bowls; nay, I once observed even a hand-made *sufuria* taking shape while a warder waited so that he might buy it. And I noted with amusement that the teaspoon was actually modified presumably at the request of the sugar retailers, who had found that the standard version — the smallest measure they could find for a shilling's worth of sugar — could yield them no worthwhile profits. So the tinsmiths made a spoon yet smaller than the teaspoon. Imagine its size and capacity — a mere thimbleful! From the same artisans also came rings, bracelets, necklaces and other trumpery and bric-a-brac.

An unscrupulous electrician contrived an appliance for boiling water by connecting two electric wires with some kind of extension coil springs (looted from the workshops) and sold many of his products to other inmates. Those inmates, using these crude and dangerous gadgets on the electric outlets of their cells, often blew the fuses, causing blackouts.

Such was the commerce at Upper Prison. Such was how the prisoners were sowing their wild oats in their prison "salad days".

CHAPTER FIVE

JOURNAL OF A SALAD DAY

How eventful those salad days,
how replete with reminiscences!

(ALMOST OUT OF HABIT) I get up about seven am. I sit up and yawn, still yearning for sleep. I massage my ribs and limbs still aching from the pressure on the hard concrete floor, and I look around. Our ward is an overcrowded ghetto, inadequately ventilated, being formerly a warehouse for motor-tyre inner tubes. Yonder, at the far end of the room is Lugard's soldier sleeping like a corpse, his jaws parted wide; and I am momentarily gripped with fear he may actually have drifted into eternal sleep. (He is a *slugabed*, though.) I hope for the best for him.

I fold up my bedding (only an old blanket I once exploited from a desperate smoker here for just three cigarettes!) and I go directly to the common showers for a wash with other early birds, so I primp myself for the day.

Every Sunday about nine o'clock in the morning, Mass is said under a tree at Soweto by a priest from the Archdiocese; he is usually accompanied by some Reverend Sisters wishing to pray for us too. My favourite anthem is usually sung: Nearer My God to Thee... After the service I feel somewhat complacent.

How eventful those salad days, how replete with reminiscences!

It is a typical weekday, bright and clear. I go under the warming sun on the playground, where other inmates have already started gathering in sparse groups, standing around or sitting on chairs, or crouching down on their haunches, prattling about Lord knows what.

I place down my revolving chair (alas, the only thing I ever looted in my life!) and slump down on it, facing the reception. I am in time to see the outer portal swing open to let in another drove of prisoners. Briefly I see the expanse of Lake Victoria (a rare chance) under a beautiful horizon. When the portal swings shut again, I feel nostalgic!

As my attention is focused upon the reception, I am suddenly distracted by a friend's arrival at my flank, and in another moment a second friend also joins in to make us a threesome of sub-intellectual conversationists. The latter is an Air Force colleague of mine; the former is a newfound acquaintance here with no military background.

After the salutations, I broach the subject by drawing their attention to the reception proceedings. I volunteer an opinion that it will not be long before our congestion reaches an alarming level once more.

The civilian observes with mild concern that all the post-independence Governments have added hardly another jail to the colonial heritage, yet they are now jailing more people than ever before.

But the Air Force colleague wittily points out that, if they erected more jails, they would merely jail more people than ever. He argues, therefore, that the fewer the jails the better: "If jails are in shortage, then, inevitably, there'll be congestion. And that in itself would be excuse enough to release some prisoners, which is what we want. Moreover, I myself never heard of a politician who cried for more jails—why? The very policy-makers themselves are potential jailbirds." (Hearty laughter at this controversial viewpoint.)

Our conversation party has snowballed to six. Talk drifts from one topic to another and finally to the most memorable event in the colleague's Air Force days: the historic Entebbe raid. He tells his own experience more or less thus:

> The time was midnight. We were rudely brought awake by a drumfire that suddenly burst open upon the airport. At that time the commanders of the various infantry units deployed there to cordon off the airport were still dancing away the night at the nearby Lake Victoria Hotel. They panic-raced to their houses, or to the nearest telephone, to get contact with their units. Alarm, confusion, chaos and the like reigned. Tempers were hot!

> At the Air Force barracks [about three miles away from the scene of the fighting and where I was at the time] the soldiers who came out in answer to this shooting alarm pestered our undecided armourer, as the Zionist guns roared on, "What are we waiting for? Give us the guns."

Then, as the armourer was about to open the store, our regimental sergeant-major (better known as RSM), a totally illiterate *afende* who was ever inclined to the language of the gutter and the rudest obscenities, came and virtually snatched the keys of the armoury and told the soldiers in a sarcastic tone, "If you want to fight, go and fight with your penises." The soldiers roared with ribald laughter, for that could only mean that they could as well go back to their beds and continue making love to their wives.

Our party rocks with laughter.

Obviously the RSM was under strict instructions not to issue any arms till further advice was otherwise. At that time nobody could guess rightly what was taking place except that another coup attempt was the only idea in mind, therefore the reason for refusing to arm the soldiers anyhow. Apparently, even President Amin himself didn't know what was taking place next door to State House. You can imagine how little the Israelis had been expected, then. Yet earlier Amin, displaying quite some bravado, had flexed his muscles against the possibility of a rescue bid.

The Israelis were chased away, as Amin preferred to put it, by tank corps expedited from Kampala. But what we all understood in Entebbe was that the tank corps arrived at the scene long after the *Star of David* had been airborne. Perhaps to bolster up the lie that his counter-attacking force had done the job to "repulse" the Israelis, Amin even praised to the skies the commander of the tank corps and, as was his wont, promoted him on the spur of the moment for "chasing away" the Israelis! All this commander did, as we learnt, was to carry out reprisals upon five innocent air traffic control officers for allegedly failing to detect and report the Israeli planes. Needless to say, in Entebbe we were all amused again about the promotion but sorry for the bereaved families of those unfortunate victims.

And in that raid, as I recall too, some foreign cartoonists unflatteringly depicted Uganda's soldiers as paper tigers or mere boy scouts for their poor match against the crack Israeli commandos. Perhaps that was the most smarting ridicule and humiliation of Amin's regime!

By the conclusion of that anecdote our company has become too large a crowd for cohesive conversation, which is soon steered round to workaday chatter and hopeless rumours. It's now even more difficult to get a chance to speak, so I am crowded out and I turn my focus and attention to other physical aspects of the prison.

I spin round on my rotary chair scanning the view until I face the kitchen to make sure the food is in process. The cooks must be busy inside there. They have been so, slogging away since dawn to produce food for the 2,000-odd mouths by sundown. I continue my rotation. The place is almost like an amusement park or some sort of resort, with crowds of inmates milling about or lazing on the lawn. Some of them are riding on the deck and on the canopy of the impounded boat. In the same scope I notice two extremely dirty and shabby inmates eating discarded food from the refuse heap behind the stern of the boat. They habitually do it. Lunatics! But I am reminded I have old food saved from yesterday's helping, and I am hungry. And to wash down that cold *ugali*? I feel my pockets and find three shillings (lucky they haven't floated yet), enough to buy tea without sugar. So I take leave of the company on the pretext that the sun is too hot for me.

There in Soweto I go to one of those "tank bistros", so called because they are under the water tank and profess to render quick service. No sooner am I seated than I am washing down the cold *ugali* with hot tea.

I fritter away more time watching inmates milling about with all that cacophony of market clamour. There is a vivid bustle of activity of all kinds: gambling, wicked jokes and horse laughs that leave nothing to suggest there is any grieving.

Now some jolly fellow touts above the babble, quite like an auctioneer: "Just arrived! Hot cakes! Made by a hot Jane! Toothsome as she must be, ha-ha-ha! Of what use to scrimp and save and starve? Bring your money to me and you won't starve! *Bei laisi*: three for ten, or ten for three — whichever way you like! Come one, come two, hurry all…"

Some inmates are washing their rags, others are putting out their bedding to be aired in the sun and to search for lice in it, or to shake the dust out. Some more prisoners simply sun-laze on the pavement and fidget in search of lice in the clothes they are wearing. (Actually, I doubt if any prisoner has immunity from invasion by these parasites.)

There are some more prisoners under the showers. A man can use the showers as many times or for as long as he likes. The national water board, I note, is the only department that never lets Upper Prison down as, I hear, they every so often do elsewhere in the metropolis while rehabilitating the old or broken pipes and pumps. Even if our faucets went dry or were running reluctantly, we would still resort to the huge reserves from the fire hydrants. So, in whatever case, our tap runneth over.

Now a prison warder enters Soweto. Remarkably, he looks all but a caricature: It is neither rainy nor cold. It is a vintage sunny day, yet he has his cardigan on and a mackintosh. He is by no means obese, yet he appears to be so. That is how he was able to come in with his contraband: There are sachets of peanuts in his trouser pockets, inside the enormous pockets of his mackintosh, under his tight-fitting cardigan, inside his stockings, up the sleeves. He is bursting at the seams! Even the peaked cap is hiked high on his head because under it, too, there are more sachets of nothing else but peanuts, peanuts, peanuts!

As soon as he steps into Soweto the retailers throng around him to buy his commodity in almost a scramble. In about ten minutes he has sold about 300 sachets and he can go out again to return with more commodities. That is the *modus operandi* of the bootleggers in broad daylight. But, of course, during the night time these precautions are not necessary. Sackloads can be hauled in without hindrance or fear of being caught.

I move on to the hospital and join the long queue of patients outside it. Not of necessity is the queue all that long, but it is so simply because a good number of the queuers, albeit not sick, would like to get some medicine to put by for a rainy day. Yet some others just prowl about there just to make eyes at the young, beautiful, glamorous sister and the florid, buxom, elderly nurse. And, oh yes, I nearly forgot, there is also a slatternly nursing maid, who often gets ignored, though she is young.

The nurse is evidently past her prime and I imagine she must have a daughter too big to be left alone. Nonetheless, the sex-starved inmates cannot help lustful feelings after this near grandmother figure. The sister, of course, captivates and intrigues everyone. Endowed with pretty features, a light complexion, a trim graceful figure with splendid sex appeal (ah, she's simply lovely!), she is the constant subject of gossip and, in a manner of speaking, the toast of Upper Prison. In fact, nearly as often as she goes by, some rowdy prisoners are fond of teasing her with all sorts of exclamations and wolf whistles, while other more modest prisoners furtively cast amorous glances at her, but she seems oblivious to it all, or perhaps pretends so.

Even The Chieftain, who evidently was a lady's man in his hey days, once in a while, it seems, repairs to the hospital to flirt with this goddess. As proof of this, one day he took his complaint to her:

"Sister", he piped up in his uninhibited metallic voice, "my backside is stiff—can't you do something about it? Ouch," he suddenly ejaculated with a grimace, "it hurts too!"

The patients who happened to be there had a good laugh, and the sister, smiling in amusement too, told The Chieftain to go back in the afternoon. It is doubtful if the old man ever got the massage that he probably needed.

To get back where I strayed from, there are more patients waiting for injections inside the treatment room. When the elderly nurse is ready to begin administering them, she first tells them to go out, with an imperative contralto, as if she were ordering her naughty children around (in Luganda).

"All right, everybody get out now and make one line…"

The sexist patients feel slighted as they file out of the room, reluctantly. Someone with a typical male chauvinist mentality remarks in an undertone with dejection, "How can a mere woman lord it over us!" Really, it makes me fancy, too, that when she is with her husband she is as likely as not to henpeck him also.

I leave the hospital, taking only two aspirins, which I am going to save for an unpredictable headache. As I emerge from Soweto I see, to my holy horror, a man—or perhaps a boy?—sprinting across the playground in objectionable stark nudity, to the amusement of the sun-lazers. For sufficient reasons I shall call this streaking character Big Baby. Big Baby, a lunatic or at best an imp. I am soon to learn that he was simply indulging in his kind of jokes and fun. Among his other oddities, the only holy thing that he does is to catcall the tune of our national anthem in the shrill pitch of a beetle, sometimes with enviable perfection, but at other times off key (A thumbnail sketch of him later.)

The afternoon sun disperses the crowds from the playground to shelter inside their wards. Only the businessmen at Soweto can brave the scorching sun to tend their wares. I also retreat to the company of my wardmates, whom I find rather a bore, as they crack nothing else but old chestnuts and tell time-worn infantile fables such as that about "Kalulu the Hare", or recite those tales from "The Arabian Nights" that we so loved at school. But to let the sun overpass, I make do with and pretend to like their boredom.

When the sun relents in the evening we regroup under it again to wait for the only meal, which, when it comes, puts us asunder again. About six o'clock the food is brought in old, rusty aluminium trays and pails in need of scouring, and it is distributed on the playground. Everybody takes his "block" of *ugali* (which takes a cuboid shape) in one hand and a bowl of vegetables in the other, and withdraws to some place to gobble it with ravenous gusto.

After the meal I join a company of inmates to listen to the radio. It is a moonless spell and the dark hour has come. At the gate, as usual, there are inmates waiting for consignments of goods from their business partners.

Suddenly, through a wicket-gate from the reception area to the veranda, two heavy sacks are hauled in one after the other by two Tanzanian guards. Following behind are two more of them, each carrying two cartons. The waiting businessmen eagerly and quickly pounce on the sackloads and help lug them to some dimly lit area on the playground. The others with the cartons are thronged in the same manner and they also retreat to haggle in a dog-eat-dog manner. The price agreed, the purchase is concluded: The businessmen buy large quantities of sugar and peanuts (measured out in mugs) from the sacks, canned beans and canned beef from the cartons. In about half-an-hour the transaction is over and the Tanzanians go back smiling from ear to ear with bulging pockets of money they have made by filching from their own quartermaster's ration store.

Then I repair to my evening hang-out at the officers' wing to play my favourite parlour game, Scrabble, which belongs to one of the inmates there. As I enter I am greeted with the usual evening recreation clamour and jests. The officers' courtyard, nearly the size of a basketball pitch, is lighted with bright neon lamps, flooding it to its very ends. After the meal everybody regains the strength and the mood for the loudest banter and laughter. A group of officers are secluded at one end, competing in self-aggrandisement:

"My paratrooper's badge, you know, came from General Moshe Dayan!" one of the interlocutors brags.

"Ugh, that's nothing," belittles another, "I was commissioned by *The Queen*!"

Yet another retorts, "More'n that, I've *dined* with her!"

They all roar with laughter.

I ignore the rest of their badinage and I locate my company for Scrabble, so we settle down to a game in the court. Another party of gentlemen are playing Monopoly just next to us. I hear one of the players yammering with mock exasperation, "Nobody's calling in my estate. They are landing on 'Supertax' all the time. I think I'm gonna buy Supertax." They roar with hearty laughter.

At our table a controversy is raised as one player argues about the spelling of a word, but the owner of the word saves the dictionary consultation: "Look here, you son of a gun," he says to the challenger as he stands up to gesticulate with his index finger over his fly, "Do you pee with 'e-a' or with double 'e'?" Thus the controversy is cleared-up amid thunderous laughter.

Soon my playmates call it bedtime. But for me the time is too young yet for the hard concrete bed and, moreover, I also indulge in the odd drink by the name of none other than *enguli*. So I search my coffers again and I find forty bob — enough for a "young" bottle of the nightcap.

I pass out of the officers' wing and proceed to Soweto to a certain publican who will open for you any time as long as your visit is pertinent to his stock-in-trade. I pass by a few inmates still in conversation at that hour, about ten o'clock. Some of them are convivially clubbed together around a bottle of *enguli* on the pavement. Some retailers have not yet packed up and are still vending their goods under a bright light outside; even at that time tea or coffee (preserved in Thermos flasks) can still be obtained (for a price, of course). Most of the inmates have gone to roost.

The door to my publican's hole-in-the-wall cell is still wide open. From the threshold I give the password, "Is there still booze in this *mabus*?"

"Ay," replies the publican, "can't afford not to have it — *karibu ndugu!*"

I step in and sit down on the floor, with my back leaning upon the wall, my knees raised nearly up to the chin, arms folded across my chest, as the unborn child snugly nestles in its mother's womb, and so are the others in the room seated so as to economise the cell's tiny space. The inside of this cell is tawdry with cheap pictures of nude women daubed upon the walls by some vulgar artist among us, but otherwise the publican keeps it tidy and snug as far as prison standards go. A stick of incense is smouldering, producing a welcome sweet aroma. Underneath the nude pictures is the publican's motto scrawled simply: FOR CASH ONLY. Not likely for the erotica but for the several canteens of *enguli* which are placed on the floor right underneath the motto.

I salute the other occupants of the room, among whom is one Captain Mirinda, an alcoholic almost as compulsive as that unfortunate captain in *Treasure Island*. He nonetheless keeps a sleek appearance, being always clean-shaven and dapper. My order for *enguli* is poured (actually decanted to exclude any sediment) into a mug, with cash down first, of course, for that is the iron-clad rule of the publican. I learn that Captain Mirinda and his companion have just drained a "mature" bottle (paid for by the latter), ready for another. Inside this cell there are four of us: the publican, Captain Mirinda and his companion and (I am) the scribe; we engage in the following conversation:

CAPTAIN MIRINDA: [To the publican, with almost a command] Give us another bottle, please.

COMPANION: [Corrects the ambiguity] With *enguli* in it, mind you. [All laugh]

PUBLICAN: [Politely] Cash down first nowadays, Sir.

CAPTAIN MIRINDA: [Glibly] Don't you worry. The money is coming tomorrow. I was expecting 5,000 shillings this evening. The warder I sent for it must be stranded somehow. In any case he must bring the money tomorrow. He never lets me down.

PUBLICAN: But, moreover, you already owe me some money. Have you forgotten the drink you had some two weeks ago? I thought you were paying tonight.

CAPTAIN MIRINDA: I know I owe you 240 shillings. But I have been broke since, because my benefactor was out of town. Now that I learnt he is back, I sent for assistance today. When I get the money tomorrow, I shall pay for the old and the new drink.

COMPANION: [Tries to lend credence to the lies] The captain is telling the naked truth. I happened to be with him when he gave the errand. The warder is trustworthy, so is the captain. [Adds rather jestingly or flatteringly] In fact, the captain is even credit-worthy to Bank of Uganda! [All laugh]

CAPTAIN MIRINDA: Yeah, that's the plain truth. Come on, just one —

PUBLICAN: [Still incredulous] What if your benefactor hasn't provided any money? That may be why your friend doesn't bother to show up.

CAPTAIN MIRINDA: [Somewhat irritated] No, I've no doubt whatever my donor will provide the money.

PUBLICAN: [Still uninfluenced] What if your man comes back with naught. By tomorrow I'll have no capital to operate with, and where else do you imagine I can make money from for the long feature (a malapropism) in this prison?

CAPTAIN MIRINDA: [Feigns astonishment] Who tells you we are going to be here longer than another week or two?

COMPANION: Maybe the publican himself wishes to stay longer than that!

CAPTAIN MIRINDA: [To the publican] Don't you ever keep your ears open? Haven't you heard we're going to start working next week? As a matter of fact, I got the tip from an authoritative HQ source.

COMPANION: I have also heard that the Chief-of-Staff is due here next week to assign us our new duties.

SCRIBE: So have I too!

CAPTAIN MIRINDA: [Cries triumphantly] Aha, there you are! I could shed more light upon the matter, but without a drink I must go. [Makes as if to get up]

SCRIBE: No, captain, pray tell us the rest of it. I think the publican was only fretting about the unpredictable tomorrows here. Now that he has heard for himself that in only a week's time he will be in the loving embrace of his wife, he should be cheered up to the mood of liberal giving. [To the publican] Are you married? —

CAPTAIN MIRINDA: [Chips in impatiently, with a confident authoritative tone] Anyhow, we are quitting this limbo back to normal duty, only next week! So what's your worry, my friend? You give us two more drinks and round up the bill to 400 shillings. Come on, we must celebrate!

The publican, no longer hesitant, fills their mug from a mature bottle and quits whining and worrying about the shape of his business and the improvident future. Perhaps he will give them even a third drink and more!

We proceed with "the *enguli* act" amid conversation centred on Captain Mirinda's news about our imminent departure from prison back to the army, to our families and, of course, the fleshpots. Captain Mirinda, now sated with the drink, almost monopolises the chat with fabricated details as the rest of us, in an almost drunken euphoria, listen keenly.

At last I drain my vessel and inquire about the time. Almost midnight. I bid the company "Good night" and walk out of the cell and out of Soweto.

There are still a few souls pacing up and down the veranda, determined to keep vigil, for they do not trust a long night of sleep in these circumstances, or maybe they are just night owls. From the same veranda I can hear the loud snores of the houseless prisoners. (Poor souls!) I proceed to my ward and find the lights have long been put out, so I grope my way in in the dark, tiptoeing by the sleeping inmates till I find my place more by instinct than by any other sense or aid. I lay down my bones to rest.

In this crowded house, where we always sleep so closely packed together, our bodies nearly touching one another, it is nigh impossible to manage to sleep: the concrete is hard on our ribs; the air is hot, humid and fouled with continual farting; the loud drones of habitual snorers is vexing, and occasionally a man dreams aloud, letting out stifled cries of horror.

How disgusting!

CHAPTER SIX

HUNGER AMID HOPE

There's enough on this earth to satisfy men's need but not enough to satisfy men's greed.

Mahatma (Mohandas Karamchand) Gandhi

THE *BAZUNGU* RETURNED AFTER several weeks since their first look-in on us. They came with the first answer to our SOS: blankets, which were doled out one to each prisoner, and a variety of games — packs of playing cards, checkers, Scrabble, Ludo, bingo, dominoes, a number of footballs and volleyballs — plus stationery to enable us write letters.

They took our census with full particulars; we wrote brief, code-like sorts of messages to our families on some special forms, which they themselves were to deliver and return with answers on the counterfoils. They also took down the necessary details to facilitate tracing the whereabouts of the refugee families of certain prisoners. They left with another promise: to bring more relief supplies soon to ease our distress.

The acquisition of blankets generally boosted our scanty bedding and improved our sleep; the indoor games, as well as football and volleyball, were soon to become popular pastimes to break the ennui of a vegetable life, or rather existence. In the same week another Good Samaritan donated a large number of Bibles, for which the inmates scrambled. They also added to our pastime by way of reading matter.

By now rumours had, as it were, come full circle. So had our Fools' Paradise, with the recent transfer of some of our colleagues to up-country jails, which only seemed to indicate that our ordeal was just beginning instead of about to end. We were, however, gratified and consoled with the recent ministration of our Red Cross *Bazungu* and their promise of more.

It was not long, however, before rumours again started filtering in with both good and bad tidings. One evening we heard a rumour, or more precisely a whisper, that there were problems simmering to higher temperatures in the UNLF Government. True to that rumour, the following evening's radio newscast announced the summary and arbitrary removal from power (allegedly by the NCC) of 68-year-old President Yusuf Lule (making it the shortest presidential tenure ever—68 days only!) and the rise of one Godfrey Binaisa to succeed him. But he (Binaisa) was least greeted with public acclamation.

To some, if not most people, this sudden switch in the Government might not have come as a total surprise. But I noted with amusement that the following morning some warders were to learn from the inmates about the new twist, a fact or a secret some inmates had two days earlier predicted or even known would happen. Never underestimate prisoners' sources of information and "grapevine."

Anyway, there we were with a new president—and a Cabinet reshuffle, of course. For our own part, the question was would policy on us prisoners change for better or not? Binaisa had come to power, for some reason, amid public resentment and suspicion (at least in Buganda). So, in one of his statements on assuming office, he lamented that, unlike his predecessors, Amin and Lule, he had not been cheered to power with any banana leaf; he nevertheless assured the nation that his rule would grow from hate to love. So we hoped that his initiative to foster that love would immediately begin with us, the most disgruntled and neediest. But, unfortunately, Binaisa's ascendancy to the presidential perch had been the least dramatic of all: Put metaphorically, he catapulted there from America by jet airplane with only an attache-case in a place where tanks and guns blazing were the only fashionable means; really that is to say Binaisa became just another president in name only! Nevertheless, in Binaisa we had found a new hope and a new prayer: Almighty Godfrey us!

So this new change ushered in fresh rumours and reinvigorated our hopes. When the commissioner came smiling reassuringly before us one afternoon, there was quite a high feeling of excitement in the air because everyone thought he was about to declare the good news. We lent him the best of our ears as he began to speak.

Anyway, his tidings were good but had nothing to do with our release: We would, with immediate effect, be allowed personal visitors daily, barring weekends, and they might supply us with any essential provisions, restricting home-made dishes. So our visitors would provide us with soap, sugar, salt, canned foods, ripe bananas, oranges and other kinds of fruits, to say nothing of a grapevine. It was a humanitarian consideration, at least, not to let us starve, and there was also a general feeling of excitement for the sheer hope of seeing our beloved ones after what already seemed to us like an age. Therefore we expressed our appreciation with a modest applause.

Probably our caring *Bazungu* had prevailed upon the relevant authorities to grant this privilege. They might have argued that if kith and kin were, in the first place, allowed access to the prisoners, it wouldn't be necessary for them to attempt to trace some of the "lost" families of some prisoners, an extensive and perhaps bootless odyssey they had been contemplating.

The visitors' reception room could not be used because the intercommunication facilities were out of commission. So the prison keepers appointed the middle gate between the reception hall and the rectangular projection as the meeting point between the prisoners and their visitors. From here the visitors could also have a clear panorama of the inner quad, where the vast majority of us were always pining away like the inmates at Entebbe Zoo; and, moreover, that in itself must have given some of us a feeling of being pilloried!

In a week, visitors from Kampala and nearby started trickling in. Then in the second week the stream magnified, in the third week, to almost unmanageable dimensions. The warders conducting visitors to the meeting point for only a five-minute exchange, sometimes lost patience and temper, and used brute force to drag away visitors who sometimes delayed obeying the peremptory time's-up signal. One such incident was opposed with pugilistic action when a warder shoved aside a prisoner's wife roughly and immodestly. The wronged prisoner, in an understandable umbrage, simply poked his hand through the gate and smacked the discourteous warder on the face, thwack!

The pugilist was promptly arraigned before the superintendent for a tongue lashing, slated for the administration of the cane later. That very morning the rest of us were mustered for a general scolding by the irascible superintendent.

Evidently in high dudgeon, he ranted, with reference to the incident, "If you knew that you were such great warriors, why then did you surrender in the war?" Most of us would not want to hear that we had been licked, therefore such a remark must have pricked the Achilles' heel of our feelings, as it were. In a fit of pique, most of the prisoners started marching off from the assembly, swearing sundry curses at the superintendent. Someone was heard sneering aloud, "Ugh, can't you see he is already drunk on *malwa*"! But, in spite of the massive walk-out and remarks beyond the pale, the superintendent went on reading the rest the Riot Act, vowing that if such a thing ever happened again, he would ban visitors forthwith.

Then, one afternoon in the fourth week of the visiting run, an alarming rumour left us utterly depressed, some, panic-stricken. It started spreading as if it was contagious. By evening everybody had heard of it, so that some prisoners, distressed by its contents, could hardly swallow their food. The rumour claimed that we, or some of us, were doomed to die that night; that a convoy of army lorries would come to carry away prisoners to be butchered.

The effect of the rumour was so far-reaching that it left out in the cold, half of our number determined to keep vigil all night long, whilst those who went to bed did not sleep at all but awaited the hour of doom in sombre, hushed conversations.

The night passed away mercifully, but in the morning a funeral atmosphere still prevailed, with a gloomy silence or low-key conversations.

Somehow the superintendent learnt what had gone amiss in his manor, so he came around to give us a piece of his mind about the matter. He first declared his ban on visitors forthwith, because he believed they were the fabricators and disseminators of "unfounded and absurd rumours". He taunted, "I am surprised that, whereas you are soldiers and therefore supposed to be men of resolute courage, you should be the very ones to be so badly shaken by a baseless and utterly ridiculous rumour." He took a pause and then added amid modest laughter, "After all we are merely postponing death…"

So ended the opportunity to see our relatives before most of us had been visited even once, as our distant families were not likely to have learnt of the opportunity yet. The ban, however, was not all that disappointing because our hopes, to get out of their inhospitable system to our freedom soon, were still abiding steadfastly. As usual, we sought solace again in our beguiling and tantalising rumours.

When the commissioner appeared soon again during another afternoon, we generally believed he had at last brought the piece of news we had so long awaited. Our impression was erroneous again. Actually, the gentleman was only on a casual tour of the prison and had no intention of speaking to the prisoners even. When, however, he went to the officers' wing, certain presumptuous gentlemen there managed to buttonhole him for an impromptu hearing, and were soon heckling him with whys, whos, whens and hows while his characteristic smile never once forsook his countenance.

Whilst he could not answer them off the cuff, he promised to present a memorandum to the upper echelons in his ministry. Some of the things they sought to know were: Why were the courts in suspension?; Why was the right to the process of the law denied those wishing to hire legal services?; When would they ever find a general solution to our plight?; Why couldn't they release the innocent people as soon as possible? And they also pleaded that our families be permitted to supply us with supplements as before to augment the meagre prison diet.

In about two weeks, presumably as a consequence of that memorandum, civilians who had earlier lodged applications for *habeas corpus* were called to and released by the courts. Even some members of the State Research Bureau (Amin's notorious spy network unequalled in their bloodcurdling atrocities), whose photographs and names had even been published in the newspapers as wanted by the police, were accorded the same legal status and released! Some regular soldiers who had applied for that legal provision were also called to the court; the court would duly acquit them, but only to be "re-arrested" there and then by their escorts and brought back into prison. We learnt that it was an injunction of the military authorities not to free any soldier. Eventually, soldiers, unless otherwise subpoenaed, were not even allowed to go to court on a writ of *habeas corpus* because, in one or two instances, soldiers who had been acquitted by the court somehow managed to dodge their escorts and went scot-free.

It was not long, however, before the commissioner returned again and announced this time what he termed the Government's policy on release, proposed by a special committee of the Ministry of Internal Affairs, of which he himself was a member. The policy stipulated that prisoners' names would be published in the newspapers in two-weekly instalments and at the same intervals to give the public an opportunity to screen the prisoners. If there was no specific accusation against someone within the two weeks, they would go free accordingly. It sounded and looked as simple as that!

Our particulars, including our occupational specialisms, were taken down. We were absolutely convinced this was for real, at long last. And what a to-do!

In two or three days, true to the commissioner's word, some names of medical corps, clergymen, policemen, students and civilians appeared in the newspapers, which everyone strived to get hold of, as anxious students would do to see their examination results. Some warders could have made windfall profits that day by bringing in many more copies of the newspapers to charge over the odds for them.

That day the prisoners who saw their names in the papers were overwhelmed with joy. They at once started numbering the days in a countdown from 14 to zero. During those 14 days most of them were dissipating their last dimes, daily celebrating their imminent departure. Our publicans must have seen their best business, as demand for *enguli* increased.

When the countdown was over, secure in the belief that they were now at the threshold of freedom, some of them started hollering out of the woods with happy good-byes. Then anxiously they waited for the commissioner to come and bid them go. But he did not come. Nobody did. The commissioner did not come for days, a week, two weeks, three…

We were all aroused from sleep at dawn by noises like thunderclaps. We bolted out of the wards to the verandas, some cloaked in blankets, and stood there huddling, frowning with uncertain fears. Some action was taking place at the northern end of the prison, and from the hubbub there we could make out the typical lingo of the Tanzanian guards. We waited in silence with bated breath, our eyes and attention focused in the direction of the trouble.

After quite a while we all gave gasps of shock, as two wounded prisoners — we later learnt one of them with a wounded gut didn't even make it to hospital — were carried away from Soweto by prisoners from another penitentiary. Following behind were another half a dozen of the same category of prisoners carrying soiled shovels. Evidently they had been called to aid in giving burial — without even a winding sheet — to the slain would-be escapees somewhere at the backyard of the prison. How many fell, we could never tell, but that left us with a real funeral. Not only for our departed comrades were we in sorrow, but also for our own selves, for while some of us had expected to go home soon, this happened!

This incident made the tender-hearted commissioner come to address us that afternoon, and he sought to dissociate the prison authorities from any part in it. In a gesture of one of his most human attributes, he expressed his personal sorrow about the unfortunate incident and appealed to us to desist from any more temptations to escape, and to be perseveringly patient. He explained to our sombre gathering that the prison regulations recommended that, whereas every possible action should be taken to recapture an escapee, great care should also be exercised to retake him alive, say, by shooting his legs to immobilise him. He said that in a very real sense they were *not* destroyers but *custodians* of lives. The unprofessional and uncouth measure taken by their co-keepers was no fault of theirs and they had no way of remonstrating with them about such an atrocity in the circumstances. Our position was peculiar in that we were *de facto* prisoners-of-war.

That seemed to be the anti-climax to the pinnacle of our great expectations. We spent nearly a week in the saddest of moods and in despair before our depressions were lifted and hopes rekindled by an abrupt call for the superintendent's address at our usual venue.

The superintendent was already waiting, standing on a chair for a dais (though he was tall) as he always did whenever addressing us, in order to command a good view of his audience and to speak to them *ex cathedra*. Characteristically too, across his nape he had his swagger stick, from which his arms hung, elbows bent, like a tired shepherd or drover taking a rest during his herding labour.

He always spoke to us as a schoolmaster would to his pupils when delivering a lesson, with a simple well-turned phrase, every word articulated, although with a dialectal flaw, to drum in his point. He rarely smiled but this time we could see a broad smile behind his dark glasses. That betokened, as nearly always, some good news. And no matter what his mood was, he always opened his speech with the address: "Gentlemen…"

When we had all assembled at last and fell silent on that honorific, he proclaimed, as he beamed, "I am given to understand that a Government minister is due here tomorrow to implement the policy on releases..." The rest of his words were drowned out by the loudest applause my ears ever heard.

When the noise stopped he went on, "When he comes here with his company you must give them a rousing welcome and conduct yourselves properly during their presence..." More cheers interrupted him again, and then, in the silence that followed, he concluded with yet a broader smile, "I can assure you some of you will be with your families tomorrow..." The long thunderous applause — a farrago of clapping, cheers, laughter and cat-calls — was ear-splitting as we broke up the assembly.

In the interval before the minister's arrival we were all immensely happy that the release policy was going to be actualised. Besides, another rumour also claimed that not only that 232 inmates would leave in the first batch, but a much larger additional number of prisoners would be freed along with them. So, nearly everyone, on the off-chance that he might be included in the addition, primed himself for departure. That evening there was a great flurry as we washed our clothes, shined shoes, swapped haircuts and so on, and we spent an almost sleepless night of anxiety.

The next morning, as expected, tables and chairs were laid out at our assembly point in readiness for the honourable visitors, but we whiled away the whole morning without any sign of them. We were advised that the minister's visit was postponed until the afternoon. More waiting. Still, good.

The afternoon also passed fleetingly until five o'clock and we were again told that the minister was still bound by other commitments. Wait till the morrow. Another anxious half-sleepless, livelong night of waiting!

The day was Saturday the 11th of September. The morning passed again with us waiting in vain and the afternoon came. At last about one o'clock we were summoned quickly to our assembly area before the tables and chairs which had been hastily re-placed ready for the visitors. They were unexpected at that time, for that was the lunch hour.

We waited hardly five minutes before the Right Honourable Minister of Internal Affairs was ushered in with a large retinue of other dignitaries following in his wake. We gave them a standing ovation as we applauded their entry modestly.

The minister stood before us with his entourage on both flanks and hailed us. Our reply was more than warm and enthusiastic. We were then invited to sit down, and the visitors simultaneously took their seats. The minister consulted the commissioner briefly, and in the next moment the latter started reading out names from a sheaf of papers in his hands, and the owners responded to them somewhat excitedly. The names turned out to be just those of the 232 published earlier in the newspapers. When the commissioner had finished, the minister stood up to talk.

He told us that it was only through God's infinite mercy that a man could be delivered from prison; that anyone of us would be deluding himself if he expected to be released through nepotism; that even if any one of us had millions to part with, he had better forget that he could buy impunity and get out of prison; that only one power was the answer: God. So pray to Him only.

He lectured us further. He was of the opinion that the murderous deeds during Amin's reign had not been committed by aliens only, as had been generally posited, but that indigenous Ugandans had been equally involved, like Haji What's-'is-Name (also in detention). But he warned us to forget that Amin would ever come back; that the out-going prisoners, in their freedom, should in no way whatsoever take to subversive activities, or else they would find cause to bring them back to prison; that those who remained in prison had also better obey the rules conscientiously, or else,

"We can finish you all with only one magazine…"

The audience laughed, ingratiatingly, taking the minister's last remark for a well-intentioned joke. But the minister's snub commanded silence again.

"You laugh," he said with a baleful stare behind wide, thick-rimmed spectacles, "but I am not joking…"

After the minister had left, the commissioner produced another list and read out about four hundred additional names of prisoners to be released, and sent both lists to the clerk to process their gate passes. But before the clerk had gone far in this task, he was halted. There was a controversy somewhere. There was no release that day.

The next day, Sunday, the commissioner and the superintendent sought to find out who had countermanded the minister's order for release. All morning and afternoon there were telephone calls to and from the prison that kept the superintendent running up and down until at last he and the commissioner and others concerned had to go and explain in person to the Tanzanian Supreme Command in Kampala.

We may suppose that the Tanzanian military authorities had been deliberately kept unaware of the additional number, and if they learnt of it, as we can be sure that they did, they should have been angered and possibly roused to a suspicion that the inclusion could have comprised a special task force of "crack commandos and riflemen" or "shock troops" to be assigned to spearhead a deadly mission against their military establishment. Therefore they must have directed their guard detail to jeopardise any release instead. But, presumably, when the prison officers went to the said Tanzanian authorities and pleaded with an assurance that they would release only the 232 at first slated to depart, and who were none other than the harmless clergymen, medical corps, students, police, civilians, amputees and other hopeless *hors de combat* cases, they softened. That afternoon the release was sanctioned by the mighty Tanzanians.

The clerk therefore went ahead and completed the gate passes for the 232 prisoners. About sunset they were discharged and some buses were sent to carry them away. As we learnt later, they were unceremoniously marooned in the city — most of them penniless — to find their own ways home.

•••••••••••••••••••

OUR FEEDING REGIMEN, FAR from improving, had become even worse and more erratic than ever. The one meal a day was sometimes missed altogether or awaited until midnight and even beyond at times. The difficulties (whether due to circumstances beyond anyone's control or the sheer neglect of the prison provisioner) were mainly in the supply of firewood, cooking pots and occasionally the food itself.

A lorry-load of firewood would last hardly a week, and if for some reason the supply was not replenished on time, and granted the auxiliary kitchen was not refuelled either, we would have to go hungry altogether. In such a shortage, the derelict boat, already extensively stripped of its deck by the tea-and-toast traders (to coin a phrase), could not be spared any longer; so it was soon sacrificed in one go to cook our food. After all, with the coffee smuggling cases most likely closed, it had no more *raison d'etre*. But that was not the lasting solution to the fickle supply of firewood.

A more sustainable solution was found that, whenever firewood was lacking and there was no other means to cook by, The Chieftain would be allowed to take out a team of prisoners to fell a tree or two from the eucalyptus grove at the edge of the prison. But, even in that case, still the problem would be only partially solved: With the wood-cutting taking all morning, the cooking would not start until the afternoon instead of at dawn, and that would entail patient waiting for the food till midnight or thereabouts.

So, anyway, The Chieftain chose eight strong, sinewy men specifically for that job. One of them—a taciturn ogre I never saw smile—was an amateur boxer as stalwart as Mohammed Ali. They were attached permanently to the kitchen and they took the same advantages in eating as the cooks did. Whenever they were called upon to render their thankless duty, they would first prime themselves with as many bowls of porridge as they could take before venturing out yonder to attack the trees. I call it venturing out because they would be herded at gunpoint by the overcautious Tanzanian guards.

As like as not the Tanzanians thought that such prodigious figures could turn out to be topflight commandos who, with sudden lightning moves, could easily disarm them. So they never took chances and never once lowered their guard; even as the loggers proceeded to fell the trees and chop them up into short, portable logs, the Tanzanians would have them all the time surrounded at gunpoint, keeping a safe distance too, lest the "commandos" should have ideas or get tempted.

Another circumstance equally noteworthy was the quick perishability of the 200-litre drums that were used to churn out *ugali*. Because of constant tamping in the mingling process with the oar-shaped wooden shaft, the bottom of the drum would soon spring leaks. If all of them degenerated to that state without replacement (which was often the case) we would again have to go hungry or eat the meal late in the night.

But our cooks were also resourceful where the punctures and leaks were not so critical. To save us from total hunger, they would patch the bottom of the drum with jute strands blended in a paste of flour, then heat the paste for some time till it hardened and stuck to the base of the drum, and then pour water in it to boil. No leaks! It was a tedious and time-consuming process, which would have to be repeated for every round of cooking. And in this case, too, our food would not be ready till midnight or thereabouts, with the portions smaller than the usual.

Occasionally, the food stores were not provisioned in good time or with adequate quantities. That too would be the cause of either going hungry altogether or eking-out diminished rations. To crown it all, food shortages were also caused by the sheer greed of our cooks and their auxiliaries. All of them, by way of a reward for their drudgery, were allowed to take away extra portions of food apart from what they consumed in the kitchen as their regular share. Because the extra food they took was turned into a profit-making commodity, they got the temptation to take away unconscionable amounts, only to sell it to fellow prisoners for high prices, especially whenever food was so scarce. Some of them even got the obsession to compete in amassing *pelf* and so turned the kitchen primarily into a bonanza.

Certain cooks had bonuses of food to sell at times, each enough to feed four men. Together with the enormous amounts they consumed in the kitchen, each one was accountable for an amount of food sufficient for five men or even more! Thus, artificial shortages were sometimes caused even when our normal portions should have been of gratifying volume. So lucrative were kitchen jobs that some cooks were able to send money back home to their families!

Occasionally too potatoes and *matoke* were supplied for a change from cereals, but whenever either of these were on the menu (usually cooked and served in their jackets), there were shortages and grumbling. The cooks always cashed in on this yet rarer food to fulfil the Gospel according to Mammon. Equally, the once-a-week supply of meat was much sought after. So, whenever it came, the carcass would be distributed thus: Almost a quarter would be salted away to be eaten piecemeal in the whole week by The Chieftain (I regret to indict him this time) and his aides; the supervising warder would also appropriate for himself a sizeable chunk, and some more yet might go as *muchomo;* the cooks also would divide among themselves nearly a whole quarter, which they would cook in a special way to sell for high gains. That would leave about 100 kilograms of meat to be shared by 2,000-odd inmates. In the final distribution of the carcass, the rest of the prisoners would each receive a mere morsel of meat and diluted, savourless gravy.

The cooks' inconsiderate greed had no bounds. Beans were equally in demand, and always after boiling them every one of the cooks would appropriate two bowlfuls for himself, specifically for sale. The little quantity of beans that remained would be mashed and soaked in hot water to produce an overwatered, almost flavourless juice for the rest of the inmates. Besides eating the best and the most, thus gaining more avoirdupois, the cooks thrived in prison, making quick gains to the resentment of the rest of the prisoners. Some of them became in no time far richer than the most diligent and successful pioneer businessmen in the prison. They also became the most resented as the greediest and most inhuman profiteers at Upper Prison.

Because of their well-being, the cooks were also envied; their position had become so coveted that nearly everyone now craved to be hired in the kitchen. So The Chieftain recruited more and more to make their work lighter, but, alas, only to make our rations lighter still!

And not only against the cooks were there complaints, but also against the officer corps for hogging a lion's share of the food. As a matter of fact, the officers' allotment of rations was always more generous, not only in quantity but also in quality, much to the envy and resentment of the other inmates. So a grumbling campaign went the rounds of the rank and file with a theme more or less like this: "Why accord better treatment and special status to the officers, who are equally prisoners and who, after all, were promoted by Amin?" One day, during yet another address by the superintendent to the prisoners on various issues, someone had the temerity to express this grievance too. In defence of the officers' preferential treatment, he contended that a man would always keep his rank whether in retirement or not, unless he was cashiered or demoted.

"Now that you are in prison, do you consider yourselves demoted or dismissed?" he bellowed.

"No," the answer was chorused at once.

"In that case, then," he went on, "why don't you continue, as usual, to fear and respect your superiors, who, I believe, were promoted on true merit?"

There being no answer in the pause, he added, deadpan, "By the way, if the devil himself gave you promotion, would you refuse it?"

Instead of an answer, there was modest laughter.

Then he posed another question, "And another thing, did you ever hear of anyone promoting a thief?"

This time the boys burst into a hearty guffaw. Someone then asked if the want of food we were experiencing was prescribed for our retribution. This complainant argued that, in the first place, there was no basis for placing any blame on the soldiers who had served in Amin's regime.

"Since Holy Writ teaches us that the powers that be are ordained of God; therefore Amin also must have been so ordained of Him." Secondly, he supplemented, "Another scripture lesson plainly advocates:

> Therefore if thine enemy hunger, feed him; if he thirst, give him drink: for in so doing, thou shalt heap coals of fire on his head (Romans 12:20).

In response, the superintendent conceded that it was their unavoidable duty and his own personal will to preserve the lives and health of prisoners, but they were also facing difficulties from the inadequacy of transport (the only means being a small tonnage Bedford lorry which had seen better days) and from the countrywide fuel crisis, which sometimes made it impossible for them to make sure the prisoners were sufficiently provided for. That, he claimed, was a problem common to prisons all over the country. Yet, comparatively, he argued, we were still the best fed and the most privileged prisoners in the country during those hard times; and they were doing everything possible to improve the situation. But to us nothing could be disarming; no excuse could lessen their guilt concerning their neglect to feed us.

Because of the prevailing scarcity of food, many prisoners, who were somehow able to acquire flour and other types of raw food from time-to-time, were compelled to resort to cooking individually in their courts and even inside their cells. Thus there came about so many more combustions all over the place that Upper Prison sometimes looked like a sort of a works. Inside the cells the prisoners were using a handy and convenient apparatus that could cook a little quantity of food. It was a small tin can open at one end; the inside of it was stuffed with a pad of rags that acted as a wick to give a big tongue of flame, and all around the pad was candle wax constantly fuelling it. It produced scarcely any smoke and soot, and moreover it could easily and quickly be hidden away at the shortest notice if the need arose. This almost pocketable contraption was the brainchild of one Bob Astles, Amin's only British advisor and crony, who was secured in the Condemned Section.

Another practice that soon became popular was to conserve food and eat it as lunch the following day, cold and gone smelly, though!

In a community as large and promiscuous as ours, there lurked its fair share of thieves, and such want as we were experiencing must have goaded them into stealing all the more. Many merchants complained about their wares being pinched; at night, as the prisoners slept, the long arms of the thieves reached out for their cold and musty leftover *ugali*. Clothes and blankets were also getting mysteriously lost. One dark evening, one of them was given chase with cries of "Stop-thief", but the wily and fleet-footed thief, who had just pickpocketed from someone who had taken his clothes off for a shower, outran his pursuers and disappeared without being recognised. So the hue and cry upon the thieves was raised.

The Chieftain, himself alarmed, sought a solution to this new wave of delinquents. The Brains Trust found it for him. He ordered that all reputed or suspected thieves be isolated and quartered in a ward of their own. So, through credible and confidential information sources, he soon had the alleged thieves identified and somehow rounded-up, to be banished to what would become known as "Thieves' Ward". There they were given shelter in two dungeons in the basement, which were formerly stores for the cleaning items of the prison, cheek by jowl with the communal shit house.

The Chieftain then warned the ostracised men that they would thenceforth abide there not only in seclusion but also as outlaws; therefore they could pilfer among themselves as much as they liked, in accordance with the law of the jungle, and he would not entertain any complaint from any one of them; and the rest of the wards would remain out of bounds to them. The total of the said thieves, fortunately, was not so fabulous in number as that in *Ali Baba*, only a dozen or so, which (by the law of averages) was still more than a few for our community of 2000-odd. After that measure, there were hardly any more complaints about theft.

In the face of our food shortage some wards were at times compelled to scramble for food in the same old manner. The Chieftain was not content to rest on his laurels after making conquest after conquest over the ills of Upper Prison. Still preening himself on having won victory over the thieves, he sought to nip in the bud this new phase of scrambling. As he sought to catch the perpetrators at it, he made a tour one evening as food was being served, with special interest in the main trouble spot—Soweto. As he lurked around there in the dim twilight, one of the food queues was becoming restless, so he drew nearer to stop them. He was too late, for the queue had already become a scrimmage. The old man still tried to intervene in the chaos to restore order but got shoved topsy-turvy in the rough-and-tumble of the tussle.

The Chieftain took this incident to the Brains Trust too. Trust the Brains Trust always to find a solution! Just as the wise Solomon might have done, they resolved that perpetrators of scrambling be banished to a colony of their own, to be known as "Charging Ward". The mode of serving food to them would have to be in accordance with their scrambling inclination, to wit: their tray of food would be laid before them and at a signal they would be triggered to begin their free-for-all scuffle. To encourage them to scramble, they would be allotted much fewer portions of *ugali* in their tray than their actual number. And lastly but not unimportantly, anybody who aspired to become the ward leader of such a ward could start scrambling right away.

After that lecture had been repeated by every ward leader to his ward-mates, there was no need to establish a Charging Ward because the food queues thereafter became more orderly than ever before: no squirming, no stirring and fidgeting, no staggering the line, no sign whatever to betray one as intending to trigger off the action. By another comparison, everyone was as patient and gentle as though he were queuing to receive the Bread of Christ. To end that chapter, charging for food would never be heard of again.

The rabid, chronic hunger also drove some stone-sober inmates to scavenge for partially rotten potatoes; and a couple of inmates with sick minds used to eat the corrupt garbage itself! One of them even made the garbage heap his bed and abode. Although none of them ever displayed violent tantrums, their oddity of feeding on filthy junk and dwelling on it like swine was a pitifully unwelcome spectacle to the rest of us.

Colonel Enguli's mind was also next door to insanity, but, although he was always hungry, he never went near any garbage to subdue his mid-day hunger; instead he had found a way to get generous handouts from certain inmates whenever they had some old food to spare.

Colonel Enguli's facial features, his dirty and shabby appearance, dusty hair formed in savage kinks, and bloodshot eyes made him a figure of fun. Besides, he was like a 40-year-old waif, sleeping on a veranda! Whenever he opened his small, pointed trap to complain of his own cruel circumstances, he always had his listeners in fits of laughter. The inmates enjoyed his gibberish the more, for his lips quivered with a tempo that could produce almost no comprehensible English words. It was said that Colonel Enguli, a compulsive addict of hard liquors, was incoherent even in his own mother tongue if he lacked his drink "to steady his nerves", which resulted in excessive stammering. Anyway, thus he often amused the prisoners:

In a gruff voice Colonel Enguli would announce his entry as he strode into one of the wards he frequented, babbling something more or less like this: "Brrrrrr yah, yah, yah, am very angry, and am look de your food, *mi na loot ku loot, NA LOOT KU LOOT –*" That is: I am very hungry, and if I see your food, I will just loot it, LOOT!

That would send the inmates into rib-cracking laughter; but the Colonel never really had to loot any food at all, for that was his peculiar and comic way of going about begging for handouts. Instead the inmates would invite him to sit and give him as much of the stale *ugali* as he could eat. As he gobbled it up, between bites he would keep regaling them with a tale or so about his past. Then, when the Colonel was glutted or, to use his counterfeit English, "fulfilled to my heart", he would depart that ward and would not reappear there for another week or so, for he was visiting several wards in turn. In that way the beggar never wore out his welcome. Instead he was missed by his fans. He was, however, a nuisance to the superintendent, who eventually banished him to the secluded Condemned Section because of the querulous noise he was wont to make near his office during office hours.

Big Baby was also possessed by some demon. Whenever he was hungry, he always hastened to the trash bin at the officers' wing, where he usually found discarded rotten fruits and *ugali*, some of which he would bolt down his throat in a dramatic hurry while the officers watched in both disgust and amusement. Big Baby, always hurtling and on the move, would then leave like a bat-out-of-hell and go to his other vagaries of amusement.

Standing five feet four inches tall, with adolescent pimples on an intensely dark-hued pug-nose, a chubby, moon-faced forehead and the rest of him relatively chubby, Big Baby was a frolicsome, mischievous imp. He was the *enfant terrible* of our community. Needless to say, he was always dirty and shabby; he seldom if ever washed, and that was only whenever The Chieftain could find some obliging inmates to force him under a shower and scrub him clean. But as soon as Big Baby left the shower, he always took the trouble to make himself very quickly as dirty again! For another of his idiosyncrasies, he used to betake himself to a kind of store at the basement of the East Wing block, where he had discovered a neglected variety of brown powder, which he would smear all over his body and face, and then emerge grinning in foolish amusement, looking for all the world like a hominid of a bygone age or some weird prehistoric cave dweller. Whenever he was dressed (by other hands than his own) in the prison's fresh white clothes, in the next couple of hours, Big Baby's "rompers" would become extremely dirty, extensively rent and quite unrecognisable as a new issue of clothes.

Like Adam before the original sin, Big Baby felt no shame but instead derived amusement in going and running about naked before us all—even at times displaying his disgusting libido! But one of the unsavoury things he used to do often was to deposit a molehill of his unsightly shit in the private shower-room at the officers' wing, to the great annoyance of the users; and Big Baby could neither be persuaded nor forced to remove it himself.

Big Baby's antics were tolerated with a mixture of amusement and annoyance. Despite his aberrant behaviour, some inmates sought his company to disport with him and to beg him to play the tune of our national anthem, which he "piped" almost always with accomplished skill like a sane mortal. He also used to amuse inmates with his frequent capers involving his favourite Alur folk songs. Big Baby made many fans that way, including The Chieftain himself, with whom he spoke a common dialect.

·············

About a week or two after the release of our colleagues, the *Bazungu* returned with more games of every kind, and answered messages from some of the prisoners' families. They took a fresh census of the prisoners.

The inmates acquainted them with our new feeding problems, citing especially the condition of our cooking vessels, which was causing us to eat our meals late. That day we had our meal earlier than otherwise, thanks to the immediate action of our benefactors; that afternoon six new drums, which the *Bazungu* had promptly sent for in town, were rolled into our kitchen.

The *Bazungu* enquired if any soap was still left from the previous supply. The cross-section of inmates who so anxiously and curiously thronged around them, uncertain of the question, asked for clarification; whereupon the *Bazungu* explained to them that on their previous visit they had left a supply of soap enough for each prisoner to acquire a whole bar, and had left it to the storekeeper to issue it to us on their behalf. They explained that they had also left with him cleaning and antiseptic agents, sprays, water brushes, brooms, pails, electric light bulbs and so on.

The message drove home. The inmates were beside themselves with rage over the gross injustice the SOB storekeeper had done to 2,000 poor, helpless prisoners. We recalled that it was almost three months since he had doled out to each prisoner just a three-inch cake of soap, which after all we had presumed to have been the provision of the prison, and no more had been issued since. According to our benefactors' statement, the storekeeper must have received more than 2,000 bars of soap. What he issued could have been no more than 200 bars in all. That meant that the greedy, unscrupulous storekeeper had shortchanged the prisoners out of no fewer than 1,800 bars. Wow! Luckily for the him he was not nearby at the time, or else — by jingo! — he could have been lynched by the incensed inmates. But, whether by deliberate design or sheer accident, the score had been evened for the motor-tyres that some inmates had earlier helped themselves to.

A suggestion was made to the *Bazungu* that they should nevermore route any of their relief gifts to the prisoners through the corrupt prison keepers and that they themselves should distribute them without undue interference from the prison authorities. They promised to oblige and left with another promise to return soon with soap and other relief supplies.

· · · · · · · · · · · · · · · · · ·

WITH THE COPIOUS SUPPLY of games, a man's pastime, if he had no other business to attend to, would be all day long playing cards, checkers, Scrabble, Ludo and so forth. Now the prisoners enjoyed their recreation merrily and noisily, effectively breaking their *ennui*. A few would be browsing on the Bible all day long. The Chieftain's favourite pastime was Ludo or Snakes and Ladders!

The more agile and younger generation spent their afternoons playing football. The standard at first was that of village-folk , with almost no holds barred, no grace, no style, no skill at all. The Chieftain, himself a zealous footballer (in the spectator role only), asked the Brains Trust to appoint a body of persons to be known as the Sports Committee, who would in future be responsible for the organization of all sports activities at Upper Prison. Some sports enthusiasts were appointed onto the committee and the first thing they did was to seek the players of the former Army Football Club (known as *Simba*), most of who were detained at Murchison Bay Prison. Their transfer to Upper Prison was requested and granted so that they could prepare themselves for a proposed match against the Prisons Football Club (known as the Maroons).

In time the committee lined up two equally strong sides, which became the main rivals at Upper Prison, and which always sparred in earnest competition for laurels and praise. One side came to be known as the "Shirts" simply because they kept their shirts on when playing; and the other side which played topless came to be known as the "Skins." They were also humorously called by the pun "*Masikini*", either the vernacular corruption, or the appropriate Swahili rendering for "beggars", as denoted by their shirtlessness.

Zeal and devotion abounded, so much so that the afternoon football matches drew virtually every soul away from his ward, business or other pastime. The rival teams each earned a fair share of fans from the rest of the prisoners, who also displayed the divisive and adversarial spirit of competition. Supporters sometimes had spirited arguments about the teams, players and games and there were even complaints that the winning side had bribed the referee to rig the match. A former respectable ambassador was once seen going about facetiously displaying a wide sandwich board proclaiming: "I support the Skins", whilst The Chieftain was a cheerleader for the Shirts.

The two teams always staged thrilling matches of some professional class; the players, who had earlier run to seed, soon regained their talents and skills to entertain the crowd which always cheered its loudest for one or other side. Later, inter-ward competitions were also organized to enable other budding footballers to test out their talent and potential. And therefrom more players were elevated to the two top teams. Two matches were later played on different dates against the Prisons Football Club. Although our players were badly nourished, in low morale and shoeless, they defeated the Prisons' side by three goals to two; and in a later game they drew three all.

•••••••••••••••••

AFTER THE 232 COLLEAGUES had departed, notwithstanding the controversy that nearly jeopardised their release, we looked forward to more releases pursuant to the policy of the Ministry of Internal Affairs. Accordingly, a couple of weeks after the departure of our colleagues, the commissioner returned to take down more names of some specialised personnel, which were duly published in the newspapers as before. Our morale was high, but this time we decided to regard the matter with a pinch of salt until the release was actually implemented.

Sure enough, after the countdown of 14 days, nothing happened after all. Instead we received more than 200 new prisoners. They were members of the former Public Security Unit, yet another paramilitary organ founded by Amin, ostensibly to combat *kondoism* (armed robbery) and other banditry activities in and near urban areas (Its members were cannibalised from the Police Force). In time, however, they had also been misused as instruments of death and torture to some of Amin's political enemies. They were even reputed to have exceeded the dreaded Military Police in violating human rights. Hence reasons for bearing a grudge against them.

As we had not yet lost all our hopes of releases, the superintendent's call to address us in another afternoon stirred-up these hopes again. But what he had to tell us was quite different from our expectations. He declared that he was about to issue to each one of us a new set of utensils and warned that each prisoner would be held responsible for the loss of or damage to his own set. (Nevertheless, some prisoners were later to sell their issue to prison warders. Somehow some of them had acquired more than one set by claiming them on behalf of just departed prisoners, who had been catered for in the issue.) This event seemed to invalidate further any illusions of early freedom.

We might as well have regarded this chain of events as the anti-climax to our expectations of release, even before the commissioner again reappeared, only this time to tell us not to weary of prison food. He also made clear that the release policy had been "pigeonholed". Having declared this, he hurried away, evading questions about the matter, for many prisoners had already shot up their hands, ready to besiege him. By now, our independence anniversary was near-at-hand and, in our own way, we settled down to commemorate the most momentous occasion in our political history.

CHAPTER SEVEN

HUNGER, HUNGER — AMID SUSPENSE

They that be slain with the sword are better than they that be slain with hunger: For these pine away, stricken through for want of the fruits of the field.

Lamentations 4:9

ON OCTOBER 9TH WE celebrated the 17th anniversary of our independence by spending all morning on round-robin chess and draughts tournaments and volleyball matches, all of which were played and watched keenly. In the afternoon we formed a deep ring around some half a dozen Kiganda traditional dancers, who treated us to a repertoire of cultural performances. Amid cheering from the spectators, they danced to song after song, swinging their buttocks so nimbly and gracefully to the beat of the drums. At a later stage the cheering was raised to a hysterical crescendo by Big Baby's abrupt intrusion into the ring. He stole the limelight from the folk dancers, who themselves stopped to watch his wizardry in utter fascination. With complete abandon he danced to the earsplitting cheers, like a contortionist, arching himself slowly backwards as he shook his body to the throb of the drums, lowering his head little by little till he collapsed supine on the dust. Even in this attitude he was still as lithe as a young adder, and never lost rhythm; he kept rolling from side-to-side, executing spectacular movements with his recumbent body, rocking his waist and belly in perfect tempo.

By the time the drums came to a sudden halt and Big Baby got up to thunderous applause, a total of around 500 shillings had been pooled at his side by his over-delighted fans. He gathered up the money and gave it all to The Chieftain amid approving cheers. The Chieftain then pocketed the money, saying it would be used to buy cigarettes for Big Baby, a notable beggar of them. The Chieftain was absolutely *in loco parentis* to him.

After the show we were treated to a curtain-raiser football match staged by the older generation: the Grey Heads versus the Bald Heads. This time The Chieftain himself, though having neither feature, was in the arena to do the honours as referee. The oldsters became completely spent after a lacklustre performance lasting around an hour, the game ending in a goal-less draw.

Then The Shirts and The Skins lined up spectacularly, and ceremoniously awaited the guest of honour to review them before kickoff. But in the interval just before the honourable guest made his appearance, Big Baby intruded again as he suddenly broke out of the ring of spectators and sped, frolicking, to the line-up. Hurriedly and friskily he shook hands with every player from one end of the line-up to the other, then off he raced again with equal velocity to a chorus of hearty laughter and applause.

The guest of honour turned out to be none other than The Chieftain himself, who strode from the ring of spectators and made a grandstand play with a majestic air to review the teams. To lend more humour to the farce, he was accompanied on this ceremonial occasion by a monstrous 36-inch Lilliputian, who was formerly a powerful motorised quarter master sergeant (with as many wives as President Amin himself had—four!) and whom, even here in prison, The Chieftain had, by his prerogative, created a ward leader. Their tour of the teams over, they withdrew to their seats amid unabated applause, and the match got started. It was played throughout with unflagging pep, the crowd cheering fervidly.

During the half-time recess, a short, squat man emerged from the ring of spectators onto the field. He was kitted out in a motley array of dress including a clownish hat on his head set comically askew. In his hands he carried a covered jug with a mug on it. His gait was also comical, a kind of Charlie Chaplin jester: All of a sudden, just before he reached the reposing players, he "tripped" over something and tumbled as naturally as a rag doll. His hat flew one way. Almost by reflex, his hands also flew up, sending the jug, the lid and the mug all at the same time flying different ways. All we saw of the content of the jug was a crystal-clear fountain. Thereby we learnt that the players had lost their "refreshment". The whole crowd roared with laughter. The whistle blew for the second half…

· · · · · · · · · · · · · · · · · · ·

IN THE COURSE OF six months onwards to a round year, the pernicious regime had taken a bad toll on the prisoners. The sight of Michelin was perhaps the worst commentary of our wretched condition. He had been reduced to a gaunt, angular figure, with the anatomy of a scarecrow. Still wearing the same suits, his scraggy neck, skinny and sunken cheeks, and thin body emphasised the change and made him appear much older than his true age.

By and large we were always dirty, unshaven, unkempt and ill-smelling, for we could scarcely afford soap to keep our clothes and ourselves clean; and with no toothpaste in all that while, our teeth had become dirty and stained, with our mouths reeking of foul breath.

We were haggard from the privations of our sleeping conditions and the torment of lice. Some of us, with hardly any other clothes to change into, had trousers which had gone threadbare or been patched over again and again. Long trousers were usually converted into shorts so that the extra material could be grafted onto the bottom "ulcers", but otherwise long tail shirts were also in vogue to screen the gaping bottoms. Shoes and sandals had become run-down or broken, some beyond any restoration, so that eventually most of the inmates had to go barefoot.

To keep nudity at bay, we had to resort to the obnoxious used prisoners' uniforms, for which there was always a scramble and which were eventually sold and bought on the black market! Yet early on, these very clothes were going begging and nearly all of us at first shunned them like the plague. The classic story of the fabled Robinson Crusoe should have been a lesson for us to borrow from — to get prepared and settle down for the contingency of a prolonged stay — as our situation was similar to his. For this castaway seafaring adventurer, rescue was un-thought of, but for us rescue was always "imminent", even if we tended to deceive ourselves. So why the bother with clothes? Besides that, we had a loathing for those dowdy prisoners' uniforms: The draw-string, pocket-less, calico pants (far from custom-made) typically constrict the buttocks and other private parts, showing their contours clearly; the trouser-legs, also skin tight, descend to the knees like tubes. In great contrast the top complement of the ensemble, a collarless shirt, was loose-fitting and fashioned somewhat like a maternity frock. The wearer would be not only in discomfiture but would also present an incongruous outline. Moreover, those clothes were believed to be an ideal haven for and camouflage of the grey lice. Who wants to look and feel the very model of a prisoner? Bah! But now we had surrendered even such considerations.

Few if any natural deaths had occurred at Upper Prison, but many prisoners were sickly and debilitated by some malady or deficiency. Probably migraine fever was the most common and recurrent plague. Other afflictions were anaemia, dental caries, poor eyesight, scales and other strange skin eruptions. Even signs of some mental or psychological disorders (more appropriately called "stir-craziness") had begun to tell on quite a few prisoners, undoubtedly the result of the malignant deficiencies, the relentless worries, *ennui* and frustration. Dysentery also at times went to almost epidemic proportions resulting in several fatalities, especially whenever our hospital had run out of medicines. A moderate number of prisoners were admitted to the sick bay, with severe cases of various sorts.

Our hitherto blithe spirit was also beginning to give way to a cheerless mood when we realised that being in prison was no joke or fun anymore, as yet another fundamental right was denied us. A critical case was once referred, by the resident prison physician, to Mulago, Uganda's arch-hospital. But no action was taken because the Tanzanian guards thwarted all efforts to have the patient moved, who died while the controversy was still being waged. And, even afterwards, similar cases would not be allowed transfer outside the prison despite the doctor's referral, or the seriousness of the case, or the lack of medicine, or other inadequacies in the prison hospital.

Sometimes the prison authorities would play-act the conspiracy together with their Tanzanian co-keepers to accomplish the charade: They pretended that there was permission to move the patient, but they also pretended that there was some difficulty or other hindering the transfer. A solution would never be found, so that the transfer would never take place, and the patient might die. They would claim either that there was no transport to take a patient elsewhere, or no warder willing to risk playing escort for fear he would be held responsible in case the sick prisoner escaped from the hospital.

Such prevarication or sheer callousness towards a dying man was seemingly justified on the pretext that prisoners, to the dismay of the prison authorities, had time-and-again managed to escape from Mulago Hospital even under prison guard! The excuse that they lacked transport to move the patient was also patently false, and glaringly so, because transport would always be available in a matter of minutes, only to remove the dead prisoner to the city mortuary or to a potter's field somewhere. Why would they make little or no attempt at all to save us from dying? Why would we be denied the right to medical treatment, which even a gallows-bird would be granted? Was it because we had no gallows to cheat? Was it a design to let us be decimated by some other natural causes and neglect instead?

· · · · · · · · · · · · · · · · · ·

OUR STARVATION DIET ALSO continued to decline further to its meanest quantities and quality. The daily fare became yet more irregular, with the untimely arrival of food supplies, for which the prison authorities always had one excuse or another: There would be no fuel or no transport, or their shoestring imprest could not afford the ever increasing food prices, or their purveyors had let them down, or simply there was no food to be found anywhere.

Because of the desperate shortage or stinginess, the provisioner was always sending cheap cassava powder or maize flour unfit even for consumption by dogs, with a bitter taste and sometimes maggot-ridden. At times there were no vegetables, and we had to make do with salted-water laced with lots of red pepper for our sauce. Another ersatz for sauce was porridge, to which was added a dash of bicarbonate solution (filtered from certain kinds of cinders) to impart a piquant flavour.

Such was the niggardliness of our provisioner that he once bought the guts of a beast and stored them ordinarily from Friday till Sunday. On Saturday he allotted only part of the already ill-smelling offals with the purpose of economising; that day we all ate them with hardly any qualm, though. But on Sunday the kitchen smelled almost like a sewer; yet some of the prisoners, already inured to eating decaying food and relishing it (as hyenas would), had the guts to stomach this carrion too, which even a dog might turn away from! By Monday a good many of them were queuing for potions at the hospital, in agonising pain from dysentery or some other kind of acute diarrhoea.

Fretting about food became our new way of life and our foremost obsession. It became everyone's nagging concern to be in the know whether or not the kitchen was provisioned, and not only that but also to keep close tabs on the quantity of the food, and to be sure when it would run out.

If there was no food at all, everyone would know from the absence of smoke in the kitchen. That would be a gloomy, spiritless time until the arrival of the supplies truck, then everyone would sigh with relief, assured that the day would provide a bite. Indeed a kind of neurosis had possessed some of us. I particularly recall the worst days, when we were well-nigh starved to death, eating only a scant repast every other day or so, and living in anxiety — as if anxiety itself would make a difference and cause the food to come, as if by mere worry we could add a single cubit to our stature — listening out only for the chug of the old truck's engine accelerating uphill to our prison! You should have seen people's faces light up with hope when it was heard; and when the truck came into sight, entering fully laden, you should have seen some prisoners literally cavort with joy like little children seeing their papa back home after a long absence.

The rumours about releases were no longer our obsession; it was now food only, for want of which we were so famished. Freedom now seemed so remote that crying for it was like crying for the moon, instead of crying for the very basic food we lacked in the first place. So, rumours about release were now regarded as wishful thinking, not worthwhile entertaining any longer. Instead substantial news was more comforting, to wit:

"What's the latest rumour?"

"We've just received a full store of *unga*!"

"Ah, 'tis far better than the usual pie in the sky!"

The Chieftain had to issue a stern warning that anyone caught with flour would be manhandled any way the inmates wished. Thus porridge was outlawed in our bistros, as it was apparent that the flour thereof was almost always misappropriated from the kitchen for profiteering. Inmates themselves could tear someone limb-from-limb if they caught them with the much sought-after flour.

Whenever the auxiliary kitchen, which had a less restricted access (because it shared the same gateway with some wards), was in operation, some hunger-stricken inmates used to stick around there to beg for handouts from the cooks and to scrape clean the bottoms of these cooking vessels whenever they were brought out for cleaning. Sometimes there were scrambles even for the wafers and fragments at the bottoms of these baking cauldrons.

The longest lasting period of hunger we had to endure at Upper Prison went on for three successive days. It started on the day the store was depleted of its last four bags of flour, which gave us each a morsel still smaller than the stinted one we had been surviving on, a morsel so small as could hardly gratify even a little child! For the next three days the store was not re-provisioned, as we languished in want and bitterness.

On the third day, the pangs of the hunger were no longer bearable. I am by disposition a kind of Micawber ("waiting for something to turn up"), and such optimistic and carefree improvidence had left me so penniless that I could not even afford sugarless tea, on which most of the prisoners were eking out to slake the ravaging hunger. I could not even find anyone to spare anything to tide me over that day when, alas, I was constrained to beg shamelessly.

For hours at a stretch I had been playing Scrabble at the officers' wing when I suddenly felt an excruciating headache, so I got up to leave. I realised that my trouble was not a headache only, but that I could not even carry myself any further on my feet. All at once I felt too that I could not even stand any longer, for I started sensing visionary stars; I all but collapsed in a faint with the sudden dizziness that had possessed me completely. Instead I only just managed to slump down on the floor and sat there to compose myself. I was glad nobody around seemed to notice the difficulty I was in. Earlier in the day one or two prisoners had fainted with a heavy fall (the way I would have done, too) and had to be carried away, and I wouldn't have liked that myself because of the stark humiliation.

So, anyway, when the seizure had fleeted by, I mustered the little stamina left in me and got up to take my wretched self to sleep. It was sunset. I traversed the playground on the way to my ward with great difficulty, my balance still wanting. As I went by I saw a number of youths peering through the projecting rectangular fence into the reception hall, where some Tanzanian guards were seated in conversation. The youths, ill-prepared for yet another night of hunger, had the strength and impudence to utter *some* bluff: I heard them calling out to the guards like the tough 'uns in a Wild West movie: "If no chow today, we gonna bust this gate."

Later I was a little cheered up to hear that the Tanzanian guards themselves had not served us with a mere sponge of vinegar but had surrendered to us "iron rations" — some six bags of flour and one of beans — from their own ration store. That night we were spared from yet another day of total hunger thanks to the indomitable effrontery of our youths.

•••••••••••••••••

Meanwhile suspense had been at its peak and at its longest. Our Fools' Paradise, however, was revived for just a brief while when the deputy minister of defence, a former army colleague, paid us an abrupt visit and took into a conclave about six elite, high-ranking officers from our own lot to select for him some specialised personnel, whom he purposed to reinstate in the army. But as on so many occasions no fruits of his visit would ever be seen. Whatever happened to his initiative?!

His visit, however, had certainly re-awakened our dormant hopes and there the rumour mongers had once more regained the foundation for their rumours. Usually these were retailed by a particular set of people who would have fellow prisoners believe that their sources were right in the president's office or in the innermost army headquarters.

The said retailers of rumour, like Captain Mirinda, who either fabricated them or were fed with spurious information about plans to release prisoners, would use these canards to clever advantage, sizing-you up for keeping a weather eye on developments and your potential to buy a rumour not only with credence but also with a drink, a cigarette or some other favour.

"Did you know…?" typically the bloke would say, "the superintendent is my next-of-kin. I'll tell you what he confided in me just this afternoon, but it is to be kept under your hat…"

On that note his listeners would huddle closer to him to make sure no one else tapped their message. But that precaution was, in point of fact, useless and unnecessary because firstly, as like as not he had already told it in the same way to a score of other prisoners; and, secondly, a secret could never be shared between a crowd, nay a crowd of over-anxious, over-curious and over-inquisitive prisoners. Then the rumour monger would "confidentially" break his news about an impending release of "more than one thousand prisoners to return to the army the following week in a convoy of ten buses".

For such exciting news, the rumour monger would be shown the usual favours, and if he was a smoker, he would already have been offered a cigarette to smoke while he released his news. His listeners might also buy a drink to celebrate a toast to the "good tidings". In that way he would benefit from booze he could not have got otherwise.

That very evening such "confidential" news would become an open secret. It would in no time pervade every quarter of the prison, and the prison food would taste much better to every prisoner who heard it. And it would for a while remain a matter for rumination and further speculation.

Fellows like Captain Mirinda and his sidekick must have bilked their publican creditors out of considerable sums of money in the long run, for they were wont to rove from one place to another peddling their fiction to wangle a drink or cigarettes on credit, and then string them along about paying!

Anyway, the deputy minister's visit had restored our hopes so strongly that they did not perish for at least several weeks, and then the rumours themselves began to fade away. What probably dealt the final blow to our dying hopes was an early morning search that was carried out on us for the first time. We were left deprived of most of our cozy furniture. The majority of the army uniforms still in some prisoners' possession were also confiscated, eroding further the hopes of going back to the army and enhancing the threat of nudity.

Christmas was now near-at-hand. Our cultural organizers had already made plans to celebrate the occasion with a play to portray The Nativity. To that end, certain actors among the inmates were busy every day rehearsing the drama, and an excellent choir was also practicing singing the carols for the musical interludes. As we were thus preoccupied with the Christmas preparations, the superintendent, to our happy surprise, one afternoon announced to us that there would be a traditional Christmas release (in exercise of the presidential prerogative of mercy) and, as usual, a minister would come to officiate the following day. What could be more thrilling than the prospect of joining one's family at Christmas! The dress rehearsals were interrupted because everyone expected to go home at Christmas.

The next morning, December 22nd, the Minister of Internal Affairs came and spoke to our excited gathering again. This time he did not harangue us; instead his speech and manner were full of bonhomie, as he cracked a joke or two, which we took as a token of the Christmas spirit and mood. But later we deduced otherwise; that he need not have displayed an unfriendly attitude this time, which only belied the closed fact that there would be no Christmas release after all, to which the minister himself was probably privy.

When he had left, the commissioner read out about 1,000 names of the prisoners to be released and left it to the clerk to complete their gate passes, but before long he was halted and told to await further instructions. That already left us in doubt whether we would see home that Christmas.

The day passed with no fresh news about the matter. But the evening radio newscasts announced in all the main vernaculars that more than 1,000 prisoners had been released. The next morning the front pages of the daily newspapers ran banner headlines such as: "Over 1,000 for a Christmas gift". Because of this publicity we were generally inclined to believe that the release was irrevocable. Our doubts were banished; our thrills and optimism were recouped, but only to be soon lost when the superintendent finally declared to us that the military authorities had at last clarified that we were "prisoners-of-war" and, as such, we should not be released in the manner we were going to be; that a mode of release befitting our situation was still being pondered over. Whether the excuse was genuine or not, our joy waned again as quickly as it had waxed. We nevertheless went ahead with our Christmas plans.

After the meal on the Christmas Eve, a stage appropriate for re-enacting the Nativity was set up on the playground under a brilliant lamp. We made a wide circle around it to watch the performers, who behaved exactly like the people in the Bible: The Angel Gabriel was decked out in a long, winged, white silk robe and quite surprised us with his angelic appearance. The Blessed Virgin Mary was cloaked in our traditional *gomesi* and *veil*; and her spouse Joseph was in a *kanzu*. The infant Jesus (*Yesu*) was swaddled with bark-cloth. King Herod, resplendent in full regalia, with his *askaris* in panoplies, was quite exacting in his tyrannical decrees. Zecchariah, his wife Elizabeth, the shepherds, the magi, a certain clown and others were all portrayed well. From backstage could be heard stable noises, bleating, mooing, neighing, braying and so forth.

Even the scum of the earth were depicted by a small gang of dirty, shabby rascals in a market scene. They wore rags and sack-cloths, swigging lots of some rot-gut from gourds, and in their drunkenness they were staggering, stumbling and tumbling, blaspheming, rioting among themselves, flinging abuses in scurrilous Luganda. Our cheeks ached with unabated amusement and laughter. During the intermissions our choir, conducted by our esteemed bandmaster, serenaded us with carols of very delightful melodies.

The highlights of our Christmas festivities brought us close to midnight, ending with a rousing applause as we broke up and went to roost.

....

"MERRY CHRISTMAS!"

We exchanged greetings with the most cordial of spirits as we prepared for the services and awaited the arrival of the pastors. I overheard two jolly buddies swapping pleasantries:

"Amin let us spend Christmas with a woman, but Binaisa won't!"

"Yeah, but Binaisa lets us live; Amin wouldn't!"

Both buddies let out a belly laugh.

After the services we whiled away the rest of the day with indoor games and volleyball competitions in the morning and a football match in the afternoon.

The meal of our Christmas feast still consisted of the inevitable *ugali*. It was accompanied by watered-down gravy for sauce, nay devoid of any meat! That day a few inmates were lucky to taste the carcass that we had seen being delivered to the kitchen the day before. Our cooks would not even spare the holy occasion of their sinful profiteering. They helped themselves to most of the meat to line their stomachs and their purses. They really couldn't care less if the rest of the prisoners had such a bad time on an occasion that melts hard hearts, loosens tight fists and enhances Christian generosity and voluntaryism . On such a day, I suppose even street paupers get their fill of the year, yet the prison had supplied the usual one carcass and we nearly starved!

Thus Christmas slipped away and the New Year of 1980 drifted in. We had relapsed into the blues and a cheerless suspense again.

The appointed census day, January 18th, brought the warders to stir us from sleep very early in the morning. At six o'clock most of us were still drowsy and could hardly budge at their behests to get out to be enumerated. There was a listless unconcern for this decennial event, and the prisoners were trickling out of their wards in dribs and drabs, keeping the census officers waiting.

In the afternoon when the census officers were about to call it a day, in despair, the superintendent asked the woman officer in charge how she had fared.

"But, Sir," she complained with exasperation, "some of your prisoners have refused to co-operate; they just won't come out of their cells!"

"How many have you registered so far?" inquired the superintendent.

The woman searched in her papers and read out, "Four thousand…er…"

"What!" exclaimed the superintendent unbelievingly…

The census officers had recorded just about double the actual number of prisoners through no fault of their own. It was the sheer neglect of the prison authorities to regiment the counting of prisoners. Left on their own, the prisoners, although they had appeared to display an unco-operative attitude to the census officers, had to the contrary over-co-operated by registering themselves repeatedly: Unbeknown to the census officers, some of the prisoners registered themselves four or five times, shifting from one census officer to another, under different pseudonyms, whereas, actually, some of them also didn't come out at all to register themselves.

Thus our census had been conspiratorially exaggerated, but what was the aim of this? The idea was to exaggerate more our unjustified overconcentration, and moreover, the prisoners later joked, that by so doing they had also hoped to compensate for the population that comrade Amin had decimated.

The next event in the New Year brought the superintendent to tell us to expect to be interviewed singly by some military committee, which was due to begin its job soon. Earlier, a Bill or Motion — I know not which — had been floated in that interim diet about instituting special tribunals and enacting specially tailored laws (which would have to be retrospective) to try Amin's soldiers in order to incriminate and punish most if not all of them; but apparently the move had been found to be not only ridiculous but also a gross mismanagement of justice and a dangerous precedent. Let us just suppose, if you like, that some disinterested law pundit, in defence of the course of justice and human rights, put this consideration before the august house:

"Let him who is without sin cast the first vote against them".

The Bill, or whatever it was, never became an Act, but still some of us feared or wondered if that might be it after all, if those interviews might be our "Nuremberg Trials". Yet some prisoners also liked to believe that such interviews were meant to bring about some releases. It turned out, however, that the so-called interviews were just another waste of time or temporising tactics, and maybe a form of consolation to the prisoners that they had not been forgotten. After all, the so-called interviewing committee appeared for only a total of five days in a whole month and interviewed only about a dozen senior officers. What a speed to conduct military affairs at! They carried out their interviews in a secluded office, and with an absolutely sanctimonious attitude, they plied the interviewees with questions more or less like these:

"Why did Amin promote you?"

"Did you ever kill?"

"What are your material properties?"

"How did you come by such substance?"

And whatnot.

In the first month they drew a blank, or so it seemed, and called off the probe, for they were never to be seen back in the prison again thereafter.

Early-1980 also brought back the *Bazungu* with a supply of soap, of which each one of us acquired a whole bar! Also they issued more blankets to all, including the come-lately prisoners. In the same package of gifts were also more stationery, and letters from our families, and a variety of cleansing agents, toilet paper and even drugs for our hospital.

Our ever-present feeding problems were reiterated to them before they left. As a result, indeed, we were later to benefit in the form of high quality *unga*, rice, beans, sugar, milk-powder, cooking fat and even a one-off supply of bales of smoked fish from Red Cross resources.

The supply of soap and other cleansing agents improved our hygiene a considerable deal. A campaign against squalid conditions was now encouraged. The toilets were always dowsed with a pleasant-smelling antiseptic agent. The dusty infested floors and walls of our wards were scrubbed and mopped clean at least once weekly. Blankets and all other clothes were sprayed with insecticides. A proper and orderly disposal of garbage and other hygienic requirements were imposed.

Some time in March our long suspense was lifted by the superintendent's sudden and unexpected announcement that a minister was due in again the following day to release some prisoners. As usual, what an excitement and a flurry!

The minister, another technocrat Binaisa had just hired for Internal Affairs and soon to be fired by the "Military Commission", arrived in the afternoon, to find us waiting.

On his entry we stood up and clapped. Suddenly, from somewhere obscure to the eye, wayward Big Baby made a shrill sound that pierced our ears as we fell into spontaneous silence, as if out of respect. As his tune came to a diminuendo, we all burst into laughter. Even the minister nodded his approval of Big Baby's caricature of our national anthem.

After a clerk had read out the names of the prisoners to be freed, the bespectacled minister, looking somewhat diffident and embarrassed probably because this was the first public function ever assigned to him or because he had already got a gut feeling that the purpose of his mission was doomed to failure, stood up to talk. He addressed every question to his breast in halting imperfect Swahili and looked up every time for an answer:

"How does it feel to be here — does it hurt?"

"Oh, yes!" we exclaimed in chorus.

"Do you want to go home?"

"Very much!" we cried out again in unison, so excitedly and so hopefully.

"But will you really go home?"

"Oh, yes…"

Was the minister in doubt whether we could go home that very evening, so late as it was, or was he in doubt whether there would be any release at all? Until later developments, the question was equivocal to us. But, perhaps, if the minister had any foreknowledge or hunch about the matter, then that was a way of dropping his sympathetic hint for us (poor fellows!) that there would be no release after all.

As he left, a Tanzanian captain in his entourage lingered behind and told us in no uncertain terms that unless one produced one's gun, one could never step out of prison. What a tall order! What an impossible condition! He walked out and left us confounded.

As soon as the visitors had departed, some warders came and told us what they had also heard at the reception as the minister was signing out: They said that one of the Tanzanian guards had told the minister straight to his face that any prisoner who tried to leave the prison would be shot. And what an unbecoming attitude for a minister, to say the least!

That left us all the more bewildered and there was no need for more explanations that there was going to be no release at all. Indeed nobody came to serve up any more excuses for the umpteenth abortive release plan. None of us even cared to raise any more queries. It looked as though the good, exasperated Binaisa, like *Ponsio Pilato* (Pontius Pilate), had to wash his hands of the prisoners this time. And we, for our part, might as well give up hope with our Lord's dying words at the end of his *Via Dolorosa*:

"My God, my God, why have You forsaken me?"

So the question of gun possession was the new frame-up, trumped-up as an excuse to keep us pent-up in prison. After the war, nearly everyone surrendered his weapons but maybe with no documentary evidence to prove this. How was it now possible to find out or prove who was still clinging to his gun or not? And how could you produce your gun, even if you had one, before leaving prison, the more so if the gun actually existed and was cached many miles away? Another Catch-22, really! It seemed as if that captain's ultimatum would stand unaltered, and our hopes of freedom would be shipwrecked once for all. And so it had taken that long, that much to disabuse us of our illusions of freedom!

After that controversy, however, the gates of Upper Prison yielded to only ten men, presumably in regard for the persistent appeals of our solicitous *Bazungu*. Nearly all of them were old and ailing men, and one of them spared from further torment, happily, was Lugard's soldier. But sadly, too, the ancient soldier died at his Bombo home about a month later, we were brought the sorry news.

About two weeks after the latest abortive release date, the commissioner announced to us again that the gates of Upper Prison would be open forthwith to our visitors, under the same arrangements as before. Need I say how grateful we were for such small mercies?

The Easter season could have arrived at no better time, as our visitors were beginning to stream in with all kinds of provisions to augment the meagre prison diet. Thenceforward most prisoners started feeding sumptuously, by prison standards, and generally our health began to improve a great deal.

Shortly after Easter we were jolted again by the story of Binaisa's downfall, which he himself might have precipitated with his maladroit intrigue and his "under-one-umbrella" election plan, effectually a one-party policy, whereby Binaisa, as it appeared, had sought (rather obsessively) to frustrate or exclude other presidential aspirants from participating. His being deposed was prompted when he tried to relieve the army Chief-of-Staff of his command and sidetrack him from being a stumbling block to his pet scheme. Naturally, we felt sorry for Binaisa because he had shown his inclination several times to let us off the hook. If only his powers and prerogatives had not been subject to overrule by the Tanzanian hegemony!

Binaisa was supplanted by the so-called Military Commission, which made some of us recoil with a new fear at first. Soon after they were sworn in, however, 14 returnees from overseas courses were released. That reassured us, at least for a while.

CHAPTER EIGHT

DAYS OF PLENTY

Then Yahweh spoke to Moses and said,
"I have heard the complaints of the sons of Israel.
Say this to them, 'Between the two evenings you shall eat meat and in the morning you shall have bread to your heart's content'".

The story of Manna (Exodus 16:12)

It was at this juncture, almost a year into our incarceration, that our fortunes in prison started pouring in. Our relatives and friends began supplying us again with the usual provisions, improvements to our scanty bedding, including mattresses and pillows, extra clothes, to say nothing of money. And I need hardly say we could now rid ourselves of halitosis, apply more lather, and even indulge in make-up. A charity-bearing visit to a prisoner is perhaps the greatest deed of love to him; it is his social security.

Our mechanised kitchen was now rehabilitated and the cooks were able to prepare our food in just a couple of hours, saving them the laborious ten hours when using wood for fuel. Even if the electric boilers broke down (which did happen) there was always a stock of firewood to fall back on if the repairman was overdue.

There was also a tremendous boost in the supply of food, as a prodigious donation of yellow maize arrived, a relief gift from America. (We learnt this was thanks largely to Binaisa's rapport with Uncle Sam.) Our quota of this relief was sufficient to afford us, apart from the usual evening meal, gruel in the morning and a mid-day meal.

A place that experiences starvation must have little if any garbage. Such used to be the case at Luzira Prison. Now with three meals daily, plus the visitors' supplements, nobody had any need to save food for the morrow. Instead, so much food was being discarded; more and more garbage dumps were established at random points all over the prison, overwhelming the erratic disposal schedule, so that, steeped by the frequent rains and maggot-ridden as they were, they made Upper Prison filthier than ever.

As it never rains but it pours, our blessings were soon multiplied when, during the holy month of Ramadhan, our visitors were even allowed to supply home-made dishes for the sake of the fasting Muslims. But what a funny irony that more and better food should be available during a fast!

Now the businessmen also cashed in on this new boon, amplifying further our food supplies. The bootleggers no longer had a need to wait till the dark hours. Instead, they came during their off-duty hours amidst the stream of visitors and handed over their wares in greater bulk and stranger kind than ever. Their traffic now included, apart from the tea-and-toast articles, rice, potatoes, matoke, cassava tubers, flour, fish, meat — even that most delicious of species, hog (thanks to Ramadhan!). For the sake of our junkies, even *bhang* could be sneaked in, being passed off as native medicine.

I believe that the security inspection at the doors must have been very lax and lenient; and at the peak hour the search for contraband in such traffic was sometimes carried out so hastily and so carelessly that I once mused over the academic notion of smuggling in a gun, with little if any ingenuity. So, therefore, almost any type of commodity could be brought in — possibly even a woman! There was once an unconfirmed tit bit — or was it a mere joke? — which alleged that a prisoner had sexual commerce here with his mistress:

"But how *could* she be sneaked in?"

"Well, one of the hospital women with a very good understanding quite simply procured her for the prisoner: She had his match dressed in a nurse's outfit and could, even if challenged at the door, vouch for her as newly-recruited. But even that may not have been necessary, for the security checks were so lax that women could simply walk in and out of the prison as they would do in a supermarket, with only a charming smile for the doorkeeper."

"Then what happened?"

"Well, the two spouses were brought together inside the hospital's inner sanctum. Eh, brother, how I'd have loved to have been a fly on the wall!..."

(But, of course, this dialogue too is apocryphal.)

As most of the bootleggers' food supplies were brought in in a raw state, our bistros were now able to boost their enterprise by offering a wider variety of culinary delights. As firewood was almost impossible to obtain, they contrived another device even cheaper than the candle-wax apparatus to cook with. Sawdust and wood shavings, which were plentiful in the carpentry workshop, were stuffed full to the brim of an old, disused bucket. The top was then sealed with a paste of clay and a centre shaft through the sawdust was left for igniting it. The furnace thereof would heat the clay red-hot, and this in turn would heat the grid iron on which the cooking vessel would sit. This contrivance would not betray itself with smoke and could easily and quickly be spirited away or simply left where it was, to be mistaken for a disused flower vase, at the approach of the superintendent to Soweto.

So, those who had fortunes to squander were always able to pamper themselves with a choice lunch — by prison standards at least: rice or *matoke* or even French fries with all kinds of delicious sauces seasoned with a variety of additives. Even fried eggs were sometimes available. I need not say that our cooks had no market for their bonuses of *ugali*. This was indeed an oversupply of food!

This spell of super-abundance also restored our traditional hospitality and bounty. Even prisoners who were not fortunate enough to receive benefits from visitors would nonetheless sometimes partake of these extraneous victuals: to celebrate *Idd-al-Fitri*, I was invited by a generous Muslim pal to banquet upon what his doting wife had provided for the occasion. Our spread consisted of, apart from the traditional *pilau*, mouth-watering garnished turkey with those rare Italian tubes served in exquisitely ornamented china. We washed it down with tankards of piping hot, delicious coffee preserved in a titanic flask. I never saw a better day at Upper Prison!

With the cornucopian supply of food and money, many more prisoners took to drinking all the more. The executioner also seemed to find no more embarrassment at his illicit adventure, for he no longer had to keep the wee hours but instead brazenly delivered his contraband in the early evenings. According to the increased demand, he must have stepped up his supply of *enguli* — enough to float a colonel. Careless consumers got drunk to a stupor. And for non-*enguli* drinkers, lager beer also became available for the first time.

The visitors' reception room was now open to receive the massive influx of visitors. There were about ten booths in a row, all divided in half by soundproof glass and with iron rods running down from the ceiling to a short wall. The glass screen had to be stripped off to facilitate physical communication between the prisoner and the visitor because the intercom telephone system had long fallen into disrepair.

When visitors arrived at the general reception hall, they would hand in the names of prisoners to be seen and wait until they were called. As the public address system was also in bad repair, a number of inmates were improvised to alert the prisoners as required. These prisoners went about the place shouting the names of the wanted prisoners at the top of their voices, using their funnelled hands for loud hailers; and this they did so spiritedly because they always expected — and most often got — handouts as tokens of appreciation from the well-to-do prisoners who were constantly supplied with scrumptious provisions.

The prisoners and the visitors met in the double booths in batches of generally 20 on each side. During the peak hours these incommodious booths were sometimes shared by as many as four people in each half. After a five-minute exchange, during which time the provisions should have been handed over, the visitors would be dismissed with a peremptory loud bang, as a signal, to allow another batch who were waiting.

We missed hardly any news and rumours of the happenings in the world outside our walls. The topic of the five-minute exchange could have been anything — even a plot to overturn the Government — since the prison keepers were unable or simply did not care at all to censor or bug our conversations. Our topics, however, had no subversive plans, I believe, except that the visitors were sometimes inclined to tell the prisoners such things as would normally have been prohibited.

Family news, of course, was of paramount concern and interest in the information we hankered for after a year's absence from home, family and friends. Our visitors were mostly women — wives, girlfriends or paramours and even camp followers. In those crowded booths, naturally, eavesdropping was spontaneous, out of which more titbits were exploited.

My most memorable example here is Michelin again, on meeting his wife for the first time in a year. The story goes that she was shocked by the skeletal and almost unrecognisable figure of her husband. Overwhelmed by heartache, she at once burst into a cataract of tears and heavy sobs, which was nothing much to write home about, really. But some theatrical inmates, making capital out of this unhappy meeting in a later farce, depicted Michelin too as weeping in reciprocation. But Michelin denied it vehemently.

Anyway, before his wife's tears had dried and hardly before they had even exchanged a greeting the harsh dismissal signal was given. Had it not been for the courteous warder who had observed their tearful, wordless meeting and so allowed them an extra chance, they would have parted, alas, without even a word!

•••••••••••••••••••

IN THE DAYS OF abundant food some prisoners feared that they would grow overweight and become sluggish, so they got an idea to burn off their surplus calories in exercises. There was no official objection to their initiative. Now, with so much food for the body and mind, hundreds of prisoners soon took to regimens of health-promoting activity. Early every morning they would begin the day jogging around the field, doing frog jumps, leapfrogs, push-ups, sit-ups, squat-thrusts and other callisthenics that caused profuse sweating.

But very soon these exercises evolved and developed into the more sophisticated oriental martial sport, namely taekwondo, once all the rage in Uganda. Instructors thereof abounded and undertook to provide coaching, some for a token fee, and others for gratis. The participants were coached in groups and for periods lasting from early morning till bedtime. They were taught all the fascinating footwork and handwork of the game, offensive and defensive alike. They sparred with one another in this enviable art of unarmed self-defence.

Boxing was also taken up by other young, ambitious pugilists, under a coach with Olympic titles to his name. Their arena always attracted a big crowd of spectators to watch them at their physical jerks, their spectacular shadow-boxing and sparring exercises. All these activities were taking place at Soweto open quad and otherwise inside courtyards away from the official eye of the superintendent.

Nevertheless, the superintendent eventually did learn of the deadly sports practice and promptly disapproved of it, saying that the prisoners should have confined themselves to the standard school-type physical education, for he was loath to make pugilists of prisoners. The number of participants declined considerably, and the small remainder that persisted with such workouts now had to resort to the privacy of their wards and corridors, wherein always prevailed the atmosphere of a gym parlour, with noisome body odours from the fetid sweat.

The purpose of those exercises, one of the participants in them once told me, was not only to keep the body and mind fit but to be ready for any eventuality; if the worst came to the worst, he said, those pugilistic skills could be applied to break out of jail. Moreover, I also once heard that there existed a crackpot idea to make a concerted effort to break out and take a powder. But most inmates would not support it, as it sounded so foolhardy and more likely than not to end in disaster. Besides, there was also an opinion that the public could easily be incited again to fresh accusations against Amin's soldiers, namely, of jeopardising the eagerly awaited forthcoming elections. So, were they to try it and were such the outcome, where could they find refuge with the countrywide alarm and hunt that would inevitably be the consequence?

As the days of abundance also provided food for thought, some of the gentler and peace-loving folk took up lessons in music and French as worthwhile pastimes. So the choir students would always be singing away the tonic sol-fa under the able tutelage of our esteemed bandmaster. Two self-appointed teachers also asserted their knowledge of French and organized themselves to conduct lessons, for which the inmates enrolled *en masse* in what eventually became a French craze. Their number was so large that the teachers, between both of them, had to divide their students into a dozen groups for one-hour periods, which occupied the whole day from morning till evening meal time. The timetable gave the teachers hardly any recess, for even the half-hour break between one period and the next was also exploited in coaching "private" students who, for various reasons, preferred to learn in obscurity and anonymity. Even Sundays were devoted to the private students. The students paid the teachers a fee of 50 shillings each per month, which was no mean incentive for the latter.

But they were not necessarily qualified nor, I would think, excellent teachers. The criterion for their appointment was merely their knowledge of functional French, and thus they became our tutors simply by default. The two, however, could not fully cater to the craze, and they had to reject later applicants. But the passion for French was so strong that the applicants so rejected searched more widely, and they at last came across some Francophone Rwandese, who gave them just litanies of French vocabulary (*sans* inflections), stock expressions and common phrases. They went scarcely any further than that and demanded their fee. Now, were such learners also contented to be *soi-disant des etudients de la Français? Oui, oui!*

A jolly 60-year-old veteran was also striving for all he was worth to learn English from a primer (a dog-eared copy of the *Oxford English Readers' Course, Book One*). I was once engaged with him in English banter, and our topic was eventually steered round to "Who's who?" In turn, he quizzed me, "Who is the king of England?" I hesitated, but before I could correct him, he broke out laughing at what he must have supposed to be my ignorance, and then gave the answer to his own quiz, "She is a *woman* called Queen Elizabeth"!

·················

THE DAYS OF PLENTY also encouraged drinking to a far greater extent than ever, so the prison authorities, with the aim of abolishing or discouraging it, started carrying out impromptu searches of the prisoners, *enguli* and money being their quarries. But, happily for the prisoners, these searches became mild inconveniences at most and never brought about the intended effect. Neither did they land anyone in trouble, nor did they deprive anyone of anything because the searchers were the very racketeers who would lose by the abolition or discouragement of the business boom. So we were merely playing hide and seek with the warders: On the eve of the search, the bootleggers would intimate the matter to the inmates so that they could be prepared for it. The following morning, true to their warning, there would be a search, and with a bias in favour of the prisoners, they would fulfil their duty rather perfunctorily by carrying out careless, superficial searches, nearly always confiscating nothing; and although they knew the hiding places of *enguli* to be always under the inspection covers of the plumbing system, they would never look there.

But in some cases the warders' warning did not come true for some reason or other. Either it was a deliberate false alarm, or truly the intention to search had been there but was cancelled or postponed by the superintendent in order to take the prisoners unawares at some other time.

One day, our ostracised thieves cashed in on one of those prankish false alarms. As usual, a rumour was spread that there would be an early morning search the following day, so the prisoners got prepared for it. The said thieves had earlier marked the hiding habits and places of certain inmates who used to pool their money in one bundle and bury it somewhere in the field. That night, some inmates lodging above the thieves' institution waited till the coast was clear, or so they thought. About midnight they came out to bury their treasure in the field and withdrew to sleep. The thieves, who had been slyly watching from the vantage point of their lair, saw what they had been expecting, and as soon as the owners of the money had retreated, they went ahead and unearthed the money — several thousand shillings!

The next morning, contrary to expectation, there was no search, and the wily thieves could not help boasting of their successful cunning, and they also made no bones about the fact that it had been none other than they themselves who had conspired to originate the hoax so as to induce those poor inmates to plant their money, only for them to reap it! The Chieftain was nonplussed on hearing this.

The next incident was the burglary of a store, which was robbed of some motor-tyres. The crime could not be pinned on anyone in particular; even the thieves themselves looked as innocent as everyone else. The superintendent, though aware that some of his own warders must have had complicity in the commission of the theft so that the tyres could find their way out of the prison, nevertheless assembled the prisoners for a scolding.

The superintendent, who once made a comment in passing that he would rather manage ten-fold the number of civilians than soldiers, complained that, whereas he had allowed us so much liberty and so many privileges, some prisoners had abused them by "Senseless, blatant burglarising." He warned sternly that such thievery could force his hand to keep us all under the rigid customary regime, under lock and key, that is. He threatened further that he might no longer hesitate to apply the complete prison code to have the prisoners kept under total restraint and repression if that was left as the only way to check their trespasses. He cited some of the stringent and cruel customs of the prison, one of which dictates that a prisoner must always go down on bended knee in humble submission to a warder whenever spoken to, a breach of which is also punishable. That too, he warned, would have to apply in full measure.

Such a prison code, written in stereotyped legal phraseology, was posted on a bulletin board in one of the wards. The punishments for the breakage of those rules (by commission or omission) are the most forbidding things that one can ever think of: One is a week-long stay or so in solitary confinement, incommunicado, without even a peep at the blue sky, subsisting on the skimpiest rations (or, in prison parlance, "penal diet") in a dark punishment cell. The other works is equally, or perhaps more, hideous: The offender is stripped entirely naked and then pinioned upright on a pillory-like structure that would not let him even squirm while a warder scourged him with might and main. Only the victim's mouth could howl anything during the flagellation. Time and again, throughout our stay in prison, we used to hear the crack of the thong on raw flesh and the falsetto squealing of the tormented man invoking his mother (as if to his aid) as he pleaded to the heartless torturer for mercy: "O mama! HAVE MERCY, PLEASE! Please…"

The rest would fade out in an incomprehensible whine, but usually, not before the number of strokes awarded were counted out would the soulless whipper call it off. Such a whipper must have been made of the most callous and stern stuff. And such a victim would usually be admitted to the hospital due to the sores and weals on his buttocks, unable to lie on his backside for several days. I shuddered!

I return to the mysterious break-in of the store, from where I digressed. The Chieftain, reflecting with ire on the thieves' recent trick to pinch the buried money, was probably convinced, too, that it could have been none other than the thieves themselves who had devised the magic formula of open sesame to gain entry into the burgled store. So, without giving them the benefit of the doubt, he at once ordered them to gather up all their belongings that evening and mustered them in the military manner at one of the angles of the field just outside their lair, presumably to read them his own Riot Act.

From a long way off we watched the old man delivering his tongue-lashing, and I just imagined he might have spewed forth such expletives to disband them: "Twas you that stole the buried money, and now you've robbed that store too, eh… You accursed good-for-nothin' thievin' rascals — scram!"

At an angry gesture with the sweep of his arm, the scoundrels started scurrying back to their original wards, and we were all quite amused, even the thieves themselves, for this was not another punitive measure any more but rather The Chieftain's despondent resignation. The old man had at last realised his mistake: He had underestimated the wickedness and cunning of the thieves, whom he had after all brought to live in a more vulnerable quarter; by merely bringing them together, he had actually put their wicked resources together, which could only have led to that grand larceny.

Well, the storekeeper had yet another requital to make for the second theft of his tyres. But no sooner had that theft and the warning been forgotten than a certain captain escaped. The Chieftain himself reported his absence in the early evening, to the annoyance and embarrassment of some warders, who would have wanted the discovery to be delayed till the next morning so that the captain would be presumed to have scaled the wall in the cover of night. So, with this early discovery, the evidence could point only to the reception turnkeys as the abettors of the captain, who could not have scaled the wall in broad daylight. Instead, according to a sound and plausible theory, the captain had only to be let through two doors to the reception hall, say, on a false pretext of going to the superintendent's office (which adjoins that hall) for some sort of audience or interview. Once there, he was instead deliberately left to blend into the crowd of the peak-hour visitors to make possible his exit; no doubt the bribe must have been arranged beforehand.

At first, some inmates felt like reprimanding The Chieftain for his concern about the escape of a fellow prisoner, saying that it would have been better to leave the matter to be discovered by the authorities themselves, instead of increasing his own trials and tribulations. But later, on second thoughts, everyone would appreciate The Chieftain's timely report, which could not have betrayed us in any way but rather might have been the fact that saved us again from the superintendent's recent threat to have us restrained under lock and key. In that case, then, he would have to blame his warders instead. Anyway, nothing was done to us nor, I believe, was any further probe made into the matter or the warders. Rather, there seemed to be anxiety on the part of the prison keepers themselves to scrap and forget it.

•••••••••••••••••

SHARING A PRISON CELL or a prison experience with a brother, a colleague, a close friend or at least a congenial stranger is one way of unburdening the weight of your cross for, as the old adage sums it up, joy shared is joy doubled; sorrow shared is sorrow halved.

Our multitude of army colleagues was interwoven in brotherhood, friendship and past connections in the service. In the one year we had already spent at Luzira Prison we, in our unlimited liberty to mix and fraternise, had even made more friends and acquaintances among ourselves. With the indoor and outdoor sports, we recreated and made more fellowships and associations. Thus, such an unrestrained condition in itself so much lightened our punishment of confinement. We could call that our most fortunate blessing. Our tribulation was greatly diminished by our togetherness because we lived like members of one clan, helping one another in many material and moral ways. Even our melancholy was reduced to almost nothing by the constant and abundant supply of comic relief in our situation.

But in the renaissance of politics and political parties after nine years in abeyance, our camp became divided into two, a split that nearly ruined our solidarity. In the days, party politics and campaigns rose to fever pitch, a good number of prisoners also declared their party biases towards mostly the Democratic Party (DP) and Uganda People's Congress (UPC), and such rival partisans were often heard in frivolous arguments and debates on party lines. Some of them even sported banners and motifs on their shirts and went about peddling petty politics. I suppose the political mood and spirit was a mirror of that of Uganda at large. For example, one self-styled stalwart, who actually claimed to know which side of his bread was buttered, once went about politicking with strong accentuations thus:

"If you can't beat 'em, join 'em! Jump on the bandwagon to our freedom: UPC…"

Someone else shouted him down, "UPC will always mean 'under prison custody', and 'depart prison' for DP."

"Nonsense," retorted the UPC zealot, "DP is a long shot! Ever the underdog! 'Displaced persons'! If you want your freedom, vote UPC…"

Whether or not there was levity in this bickering, some of us were made to believe that suffrage was extended to prisoners too, till the superintendent himself dispelled the conviction, saying, in no unclear terms, that political involvement of whatever nature and to whatever degree was out of keeping with any prison regime, and the bickering was curbed forthwith.

During that spell, however, by some good fortune, I struck up an acquaintance with one fellow I shall introduce as Colonel Mambo. Colonel Mambo, an alumnus of Sandhurst, with a flattering beard on a handsome face, was a witty, inkhorn conversationist, satirist and ironist. He indulged moderately in the pipe, and political jokes were his staple of discourse, although, the cynic and wag that he was, he avowed that he was a staunch non-partisan because all the parties (particularly DP), even in this space age, were still promising nothing more than a hoe instead of another planet. And his favourite "social" or "bar" joke was: "I have to belong to the bar so as also to be called a learned friend; and, after all, I only drink to live." So Colonel Mambo, the punster, declares in his baritone voice.

My acquaintance with Colonel Mambo was fostered on games of Scrabble, and we soon grew to be on speaking terms and gradually progressed to sharing jokes and even confidences. Thus, without being a snob or a sycophant, I readily warmed to his company and enjoyed every moment of it.

Every so often I had the pleasure of an opportunity to chat to him, and I vividly recall another evening when, with a third and a fourth player, both political buffs too, we fell into another gossip session as the game proceeded. I am still the legendary scribe, and here follows yet another dialogue:

Col Mambo: [After overhearing both optimistic and pessimistic views and remarks about our situation by another party in conversation near us, is prompted to point out to our company] All the parties have promised to release prisoners, but methinks this is possible with only one particular party.

Third Player: [Tries a guess] That's DP, I suppose.

Col Mambo: Wrong. With no military wing DP is impotent. Don't you see that we could merely go back to experience the Binaisa episode again?

Fourth Player: Poor Binaisa; his umbrella could not even shelter him!

Third Player: He really got a raw deal for his pains, in contributing so much to the liberation struggle, as someone once put it, 'By waging the diplomatic offensive with his pen'!

Col Mambo: [Supplements] Moreover, in America! [All laugh]

Scribe: So what's your opinion, Colonel?

Col Mambo: You realise, of course, we're sheer hostages, but once Obote is in power, we shall no longer be worth a king's ransom. Therefore he'll waive us as bad debts. And, moreover, quite a golden opportunity presents itself for him to display and boast of magnanimity.

Fourth Player: But do you think the elections will take place as planned?

Col Mambo: It is difficult to tell. But Obote will want to go down in history as the first ousted African president to make a comeback—by hook or by crook. And Tanzania is bent on sponsoring him—their secondary motive for the liberation.

Scribe: What would become of our career? Would he reinstate us? [Everyone in the court falls silent as loud echoes of gunfire ring out in the distance, almost a daily occurrence, in fact].

Fourth Player: [Breaks the silence] There goes another murder!

Col Mambo: [Corrects the improper diction] No, no, no, those are not murders; those are simply *killings*. [All laugh]

Scribe: [Importunately] You haven't answered my question.

Col Mambo: [Lights his pipe] Ah, would he reinstate us? Ah, well, the jury is still out on that. Whose turn to play…

· · · · · · · · · · · · · · · · · ·

During this period too, certain sanctimonious people known as *Balokole* (our latter-day puritans, otherwise "born-again" Christians) began going about the wards preaching the Word of God to fellow prisoners, with revivalist and evangelical zeal: fiery homilies, exegeses and orgies of praying. Here is a specimen sermon:

> Dear friends, we have languished here one year so far. The whole year we've been making fools of ourselves. The whole year round we've deceived ourselves with false rumours about our release. The whole year, day after day, we've hoped against hope. The whole year we've taken our release from here for granted, to come simply at the whim of our earthly powers. Can't we realise, in the first place, that God's own wrath has been visited on us? Who, then, can undo what God has done but Himself?…

> The whole year our hopes have come to nothing. We've seen three abortive attempts to release us, yet, in spite of all that, we continue ever to be so upbeat in a state of a Fools' Paradise. This devil-may-care business as usual: booze, rumour-mongering and gossiping still remain our preoccupation and pastime after all. The anxiety and wishful thinking about getting out of here is our number one priority, as if that were the greatest thing that could ever happen in life, as though stepping out there were the Hereafter reward. But the question I want to put to you is, will your anxiety and wishful thinking sway God's will without even a prayer?…

> If we open at Romans, Chapter nine, Verse 14…What does it say: 'Does it follow that God is unjust? Of course not. Take what God said to Moses: *I have mercy on whom I will and I show pity on whom I please*. In other words the only thing that counts is not what human beings want or try to do but the mercy of God. For in Scripture He says to Pharaoh: *It was for this I raised you up; to use you as a means of showing my power and to make my name known throughout the world*.' In other

words when God wants to show mercy, He does and when He wants to harden someone's heart He does so…'.

So, then, if God wanted to show His power to His people in their bondage through the adamant Pharaoh, does it not follow, therefore, that through our own obdurate leaders He wants to make Himself known to us?…With three vain attempts to release us, isn't it more than abundant proof that only God's power and will reigns supreme — that our deliverance from here is possible only through His intervention?…Did we really heed that Honourable Minister's advice that we need to pray to God only, for His mercy?…Those were no idle words and he certainly knew what he meant. If you didn't grasp the meaning, it is simply this: Rulers are merely God's puppets on earth, for their actions and decisions are sponsored and controlled by Him alone. So, then, how much more, in such a plight as ours, do we need Him — above all else?…Yet a good many of us have backslid into nothing but shameless apostasy and intemperance!

God put Pharaoh under duress of ten plagues in attempts to deliver His people from bondage. Our own masters are not under plagues, not under duress of any kind, and so far only three attempts have been made to rescue us. For 40 years were the Israelites in Egyptian captivity. So far only one year have we been in captivity. So, Gentlemen, what a long way we may still have!

There was moderate laughter at the quip.

Be that as it may, what we need above all else is the salvation of our souls. Deliverance from sin and its everlasting punishment is far more profitable than deliverance from jail, this fleeting earthly penalty. Our Lord taught us that whoever loses his life finds it and whoever finds his life loses it. Still, in the words of our very Master: 'What will it profit a man if he should gain the whole world and lose his soul?' How can we, then, value the pleasures of a fleeting life above those of an everlasting one?

Dear Brothers, today let's resolve to give up our vain and fruitless pursuits and dedicate ourselves to our beloved Maker in daily communion with Him. Let us bear our cross here with devout prayer and with the patience of Job. We should no more waste our time entertaining the Fools' Paradise here or relishing the prospects of the one outside these walls. We must bear in mind that this life is not the be-all and end-all. Therefore, let us first seek but salvation, for by that we may profit the Eternal Kingdom of God, that Everlasting City of Heaven. That is the Promised Land to pray for, sing about, dream about and look forward to, instead of the crazy world outside this pen where Satan has countless devices and tricks to ensnare and enslave people…

So concluded our fire and brimstone preacher. Then, to complement the sermon, they (the sermoniser and the congregation) would recite petitions relevant to our situation, such as the stock prayer: "O God of Hosts, if it be possible let this chalice pass from me, not as I will but as Thou wilt…" And they would chant songs of praise or of damnation: "They shall cry and cry and gnash their teeth…"

Such was how the prisoners were edified, and the hitherto lapsed or passive believers were inspired to renew their religious zeal with an aura of self-righteousness too. There was a wave of new converts who took the floor and declared their faith. Some of them made public confessions and gave accounts about their criminal and sinful past. They even cited instances of theft, adultery and so forth; others confessed their activities in witchcraft, superstition and other ungodly deeds; they professed their penitence, renouncing Satan and his crew, and pledged their resolve to keep a new discipline of devout prayer and constant devotion to God.

Generally, religious commitment now took the place of our obsession with rumours; it became the new soothing balm to our distress. There was once a comic rumour that even Captain Mirinda had renounced drink and had joined the pious *Balokole*. But, no, it was refuted, and it was observed that the captain simply "drinks and prays!"

And a 40-year-old sergeant-major reeled off his testimony thus:

> On the advice of my witch-doctor for the mortal evil I was planning to inflict on certain enemies of mine, I used to play with—thingummy-bob—what do you call that…er…species of frog with long spindly legs that leaps high and far like a flea?…Well, that was the creature I was supposed to arrest without fail, so that, with its aid, my witch-doctor could go ahead to have my enemies bewitched unto

death. But I was warned that if I failed to carry out the witch-doctor's orders, I or any other member of my family could suffer dire, even fatal, consequences.

Realising that I had committed myself entirely to the league of Satan, and with my strong conviction that the witch-doctor's orders were irreversible and must be carried out to the letter, I went ahead after the frog. Gentlemen, it is up to you yourselves to imagine what a hard time I had, with such a corpulent body as I used to have and with my sluggish speed, to take prisoner such an evasive creature!

The congregation laughed heartily, for this was another man who would probably have tipped the scales at no less than Michelin at the time they entered prison; but now only a pathetically emaciated figure stood before them. This was actually the man with a "ten-gallon" hat, which he had given up too! "Ahem," he cleared his windpipe again when the laughter had stopped and resumed his oratory,

but the other day I had a vision in which an Angel of God seemed to urge me to give up my association with the Devil in favour of a new one with the Angels of God. In obedience I have even dispatched orders back home that the amulets on my children be stripped off them; those counterfeit shrines to my former deities must also be destroyed, for I have joined a new and authentic league of the Angels of God. To them only have I commended myself and my family for our protection and welfare. So, dear Brethren, if thou art not yet saved, go and do thou likewise…

We had gone to prison without a prayer, but inside there we rediscovered God. What could once have been described as the Devil's Brigade, was now a God-fearing people. The community prayers (in the gift of tongues), the private devotions and the high-spirited gospel songs all over the place, indeed imparted a holy flavour to Upper Prison.

One afternoon in the spell of our reconciliation with God, the Lord sent us three ministers—this time from the pastoral ministry—in the persons of the Catholic Cardinal, Anglican Archbishop and Muslim Chief Khadi.

The long-robed men took us by surprise when an abrupt call brought us to our assembly area. Their entry was applauded with an unusual fondness. Everyone thronged together and strived to reach them for a bear hug, a handshake, a ritual kiss on the brass ring, a bowing curtsy or some other reverent gesture, all amid excited clamour. The commotion was brought to order and silence, and His Eminence began to speak on behalf of his ecumenical company:

> Dear Brothers in Christ, we bring you very dear greetings and regards from the brethren at large. We have come to see you by kind permission of our Government leaders. We have followed your plight with zealous concern and have always remembered you in our prayers. [Applause.]
>
> Do not mope or pity yourselves for being here because the situation in which you are is sheerly a divine visitation, which God seemingly sends to His most beloved, like His most faithful servant Job or His very own beloved son Jesus. Out of evil may come good: Great men and saints have been known to emerge from prison; therefore I expect that from you too will come great men and saints…

There was another round of applause but I found no solace in that and I rather felt flattered, for I had no faith anything good could come out of prison. Then the Cardinal concluded in jest, amid further applause,

> Sooner or later you will be going home to your families and, please, when you kill the fatted-calf, do not forget to invite us to share in the feasts of your joys, too.

So saying, he bade the congregation kneel for his benediction, at the end of which we chorused, "Amen." The leave-taking was as dramatic as the reception. Farewells were waved till the last prison doors closed upon the holy men. The pastors' visit and speech provided grounds for fresh hopes and a new foundation for fresh rumours. Many of us flattered ourselves that they had been to the Government leaders to intercede for the prisoners, and so had come to hint to us that our release was on the horizon. We dwelt on that hope so strongly. It was ironic that the chief religious ministers had swung our minds and hearts back to our Fools' Paradise, which we had renounced at the exhortation of our own preachers of eternal damnation.

CHAPTER NINE

WE MAKE LIFE GAY

The life without festival is a long road without an inn.

Democritus Abdera

THE TWIN DOORS WERE flung open and revealed a spectacular array: The bride was decked out in a star-spangled, sparkling ivory silk robe and veil; and her shoes and gloves gleamed snow-white. The onlooking crowd was ravished by her beauty. The bridegroom was in the traditional outfit: a white *kanzu*, below whose hem peeked the cuffs of black trousers worn underneath; and over the *kanzu* he wore a coat matching the trousers. The handsome groom smiled, obviously satisfied with his choice of bride. The rest in the pageant were also in ceremonial finery, just as in any other wedding gala.

Now the newlyweds clutched each other arm-in-arm, having just been pronounced man and wife, and led the procession to a garden party reception, where they took seats with ceremonial decorum. The bride's team of kith and kin sat by her flank vis-à-vis the bridegroom's team, who likewise occupied positions by his flank.

The rest of the proceedings were a comic travesty, in which the members of both sides stood up to speak, vying in laughter-provoking pleasantries and rhapsodic compliments for their children's marriage, but they were interrupted now and again by mistimed, uncalled-for laughter from some stubborn, rowdy buffoon, who had to be hushed now and again by the groomsman…

The germ of the idea to stage such extravaganzas at Upper Prison came from Colonel Mambo: Occasionally there used to be nighttime ballroom dances at the Prison Mess, just within spitting distance. The loud music of the dance band always intrigued the inmates in sleepless fantasies and wistfulness. Colonel Mambo, an ardent lover of music and dance, schemed secretly to compensate for this unattainable desire and prepared a surprise for the inmates.

Whenever there was a dance at the Prisons Mess, the inmates would learn of it in advance from the warders. On one Saturday that there was going to be such a dance, Colonel Mambo, now an impresario of a sort, also put out his playbill:

DANCE, DANCE, DANCE.\
VENUE & TIME: EAST WING 8.00PM.\
NO CHARGE. COME ONE, COME ALL!

This strange notice aroused interest, and when the time came the inmates streamed to the venue *en masse* to get proof of the event. The courtyard of East Wing was crammed by so thick a crowd that there was no more standing room left. The doorway was also jammed by another thick crowd unable to get inside, and yet more prisoners were content to stand outside for hours to listen to the nostalgic music.

The musicians the Colonel had assembled and engaged for a jam session, it turned out, were the former players of the Army Jazz Band, who now stood there destitute of string, brass, woodwind or percussion instruments, to entertain their colleagues with great passion. In their beautiful voices only, they belted out number after number of the Lingala pop hits of the day. Every song was delightful and cheered with enthusiastic acclaims and demands for an *en core*.

About one o'clock in the morning the dance at the mess ended; but the inmates kept coaxing and pestering the *a capella* band for more songs to outplay the other dance band, till at last they became too weary to go on at about 3 am. The show was applauded with a medley of shrill cat-calls, bleating, lowing, barking, baying, horse laughs and so forth, as the inmates dispersed for sleep. At that time Upper Prison must have been the noisiest place in its time zone, and I feared that the hub-bub would stir awake the irascible superintendent and bring him promptly to us from his nearby quarters for denouncement, but nobody came, nor was there any complaint afterwards.

We Make Life Gay

Our weekdays were taken up, every minute of them, in waiting for and seeing our visitors, which was quite exciting and time consuming. But during the weekends, with no visits, we generally felt desolate and bored stiff. So our Brains Trust members devised a diversion to amuse and entertain ourselves during the long weekend hours. Moreover, it was also generally thought that with the not-far-away elections successfully concluded, our tale of weal and woe here would come to a happy and sudden end, for every presidential candidate had promised unqualified pardons to the prisoners; so we should make the best of the final days for a memorable stay together before parting company.

The Sports Committee was fittingly assigned the task of organizing our weekend entertainments. To that end, therefore, the enthusiastic inmates were organized in their ethnic groups so that they could plan and rehearse their cultural shows for the weekends ahead. To add to what had been salvaged from Makindye Barracks, our visitors supplied more costumes, including the wedding gear in the marriage that was never to be consummated. The superintendent readily rubber-stamped the plan for these concerts to take place although he must have imposed a time limit.

Every Saturday and Sunday the Sports Committee would display a playbill to proclaim the programmes of our variety shows, which would present folk dances, songs, plays, wrestling matches, stunts, skits, slapstick and other acts of buffoonery, such as an Etesot heaving awkward strides under the weight of a three-kilogramme hydrocele; a Muganda dancing so lithely and adroitly on four-foot-high stilts; a big muscular Musoga hoisting above his head a five kilogram drum in the clutch of his teeth, just as a crane on a bulldozer would do; and a grey haired police officer in uniform appearing so grotesque that, with an exceedingly bloated stomach and unsymmetrical correspondence of his buttocks, he looked as though he were a not-yet-quite finished creation of a clumsy amateur taxidermist. What a caricature — and good copy too for the comic press!

Every tribal group was soon ready with several shows to present, but the two days in a week could never accommodate all those planned, so that it was always necessary to carry some of them forward. The feminine roles in our stage dramas were assigned to young, smooth-faced, handsome boys, who wore skirts and blouses, under which they stuffed various sorts of falsies for breasts.

Saturday and Sunday mornings were occupied by chess and draughts tournaments and volleyball matches. After the mid-day meal, we would all gravitate to Soweto, the venue for our shows (but, of course, ensuring one man or two stayed behind in each ward to guard against thieves). There, in an area partly shaded by a tree, the inmates sat and stood around in a wide circle, most of them directly under the glare of the sun. A gap was left in the circle to allow the performers' entry and exit, and a nearby ward was improvised as the backstage or dressing room. The Chieftain, flanked on both sides by his peers and aides, always took the place of honour in the cool shade of the tree and commanded due respect for the shows. The stage was set. Our premiere show began.

The Battle
The twin doors flew open and eight savage-looking men with tattooed faces came rushing forward in a wild pageant. Their garb of loincloth, something little more than the biblical fig leaf, screened not much more than the genital area, and they exuded savage prowess in a warlike mood, wielding long heavy sticks. They wore anklets of miniature brass bells which tinkled as they danced in rhythm, producing something like the chime of a carillon.

Now they paraded in two close ranks before the distinguished spectators and bowed to them. His Highness The Chieftain acknowledged their gesture with pomp and ceremony.

Then the troupe withdrew a little and immediately broke into a song and dance routine, raising and lowering their sticks in a rhythmic pattern with the rise and fall of the feet. But the dance was only a brief prelude to something else. Suddenly, the savages flared up into fierce duels and displayed a hair-raising battle royal in the traditional art of waging war with staves, a culture akin to and as ancient as fencing in Europe. The clashes of the sticks were breathtaking, as blows were fended off. The manoeuvres of the sticks were impressively swift, and all the warriors were parrying, dodging and ducking under them with consummate skill and tactics. It was a spectacle no less exciting than a boxing match! But in the end all the gladiators bowed out unscathed amid a roar of applause.

Christmas (A Play)

The cast, a married couple, are very ordinary folk in a traditional rural setting and lifestyle. The husband arrives home in the late afternoon and deposits a bundle, of which he tells his wife, "It is for Christmas." He wanders off again for booze and returns later, almost in time to find another man take leave of his wife!

A noisy wrangle ensues between the husband and the wife. Apparently the wife has been so easily duped by some wayfaring impostor, to whom she has given the now missing bundle. In the next moment the husband goes on the rampage and spanks his daft wife in spite of her defensive pleas: "I gave it to Christmas. He came for it just before you returned…" The act ended suddenly amid a fit of laughter from the audience.

For Our Ears Only

"…The war between Uganda and Tanzania still rages on. According to reports reaching our desk, the Tanzanians have pressed their offensive well beyond the major southern town of Masaka, long fallen to them. Now they are shelling the cities of Kampala and Entebbe with heavy, long-range artillery. As the chips come down, the Ugandan soldiers are turning tail for dear life. The civilians could not be less scared. Droves of them are deserting their jobs to seek refuge upcountry."

"Meanwhile, in Kampala a military spokesman has declared a dusk-to-dawn curfew, with rigid restrictions — even the use of electric lighting at night is prohibited. What the outcome of the war will be is still difficult to predict, but, as it appears, the odds are entirely against dictator Idi Amin who, as he desperately sues for peace now, has even admitted he may have to share his breakfast with the enemy the next morning from now. You are listening to transmissions to Africa from *Radio Deutsche Welle*…"

No doubt that purported to be an excerpt from the war bulletins. In spite of ourselves, we applauded the brilliant parody by a voice in Swahili from an unseen announcer with a simulated loudspeaker.

A Divertissement

During intermissions a stand-up comedian regaled us with droll monologues, such as the ribald anecdote from his reminiscences when in the employ of a certain local Asian. (In fact this was the clown who earlier entertained us with a tumbling act during a football match half-time recess.)

He began, "Patel owned a bus and I was a member of its crew. One day I was directed to display a signboard to the effect that the front door of our bus could not be used…" He recited Patel's directive in the precise words, mimicking the humorous Indian nasal twang, which already provoked a bout of laughter.

"After painting the sign on a slat of wood," he went on, "I carelessly mislaid it face down on one of the bus seats, before the paint had dried. The same impression was left on the bus seat, and before it had gone dry, too, a beautiful attractive passenger accidentally sat on it. The same copy in turn caught on her imposing derriere (how provocative!):

> FRONT DOOR JAMMED
> ENTER FROM THE REAR.

The Omnibus Dance

The real humdinger came when Big Baby led a troupe of his Alur folk dancers amid wild cheers as he entered the stage with his frolicking and spell-binding caper. Ignoring protocol and the requirement to curtsey to The Chieftain, he went straight for his hand and tugged him along to join in the dance. The Chieftain did, as did his peers and aides, and then nearly the whole audience of rank and file joined in the fun *en masse*. That left only a handful of onlookers watching the popular caper, called *Agwara*, which is executed by raising and stomping the feet alternately while the flexed haunches gyrate in a comic manner, to the loud blare of a gigantic, primitive horn. They danced in a jumbled tumult with rapture and utter relish for about half an hour before the shrill call of a whistle broke up the show for football…

In spite of the superintendent's limitation, however, the revelry went on indefinitely into the night. After the evening meal, night life began at Soweto. The night spot came to be known as Sodom and Gomorrha. It was in an open area lighted by a fluorescent tube decorated with blue and red ribbons. Three vocalists, accompanied with a drum, noisily entertained our youngsters with East African coastal Taarab.

To lend an erotic touch to the night, the boys in girls' clothing conducted themselves like those seductive scarlet women; they even giggled as the girls do in flirtation and picked dancing partners. What great fun! The one with crimp, glossy hair, wearing make-up for the occasion, could have won a beauty contest. And, for the first time, it was whispered that there might even be partners at "gay" orgies. There was, of course, *enguli* galore sold right there to make the revellers more euphoric to carry on with their carnival till the wee hours…

After a succession of about five weekends of such hilarious activity and engagement, the long-awaited elections were deferred for a further three months. By now our patience had been strained to the limit. Three months meant there was another eon to go, and earlier suspicions were fortified that elections would not take place after all. Our ardour for merriment flagged. The gay life was consumed. Before we had recovered from this blow, they dealt us yet another by barring our visitors again. So, sadly, our plethora of provisions had come to a sudden halt! That was the unkindest cut! Some of us must have felt a wrench of the heart too at the thought and prospect of never going to see our beloved ones, for however long! We were left heartbroken and bereft! We marked the independence anniversary, the second in prison, with our flag at half mast, so to speak.

A week or so later, we were visited by a high ranking Protestant minister, and so we gathered eagerly to hear his "good and comforting" words. What did he do but chide us for "overkilling" during Amin's term! After a prayer and a salutation, the bishop looked smilingly around the non-denominational flock about him and, in a soft-spoken voice, declared, "Ah, you really killed and killed overmuch. Ah, I can see that for all this prison life, you are still bursting with health. Ah, look at my friend The Chieftain: His paunch is still intact! Ah, but you people really killed…"

If that prelate actually meant this as a joke, it was in bad taste and unbecoming of a religious personage; and before he concluded his trenchant if gentle rebukes, nearly the whole audience had walked out, beside themselves with revulsion. But Colonel Mambo, who heard him out, was by no means disheartened. He merely observed what was happening with his characteristic tongue-in-cheek humour. He thought the minister, who himself had served during Amin's regime, without ever deserting, as nominal Bishop-at-Large of the armed forces, had been merely paying his belated compliments to his former colleagues; for, in fact, the bishop might as well have thought that the tendency and capacity to overkill was the quintessence of good soldiering! He was to return a few weeks later to administer sacraments to the faithful and, as I learnt, he ate his words in a profuse apology.

• • • • • • • • • • • • • • • • • •

As the days progressed, in early November, one stormy, blacked-out night when all the Argus eyes of the watchtowers should have been blinded, seven men, including a captain, made a daring escape in this inclement if propitious weather. This was discovered when the escapees should have already popped champagne to their daredevil freedom mission.

In fact, according to some other inmates who had attempted to go along, a contingent of some 40 prisoners had planned to escape that night but most of them backed out in the blinding rainstorm, which threatened to impede a quick getaway. The intrepid seven, however, went ahead, choosing their exit, by irony the most improbable and the most unexpected, yet the easiest route, right by the watchtower over the reception hall, which was left unmanned in the tempest.

Climbing to the single storey roof with the aid of the supporting columns should not have taken them a great deal of effort, and they needed hardly any more aids; they were easily able to wriggle through the barbed wire coils without undue haste or entanglement. Once that obstacle was surmounted, they had only to leap down from the low roof over the Reception Hall, where the fencing wall does not enclose the building but instead connects with it at its outer angles. That meant they had no further obstacle to overcome, but nearby where they landed was a bivouac of sleeping Tanzanian guards, past whom they tiptoed.

The consequences were left to the rest of the inmates to bear. That very morning we were mustered for a meticulous head count to find out how many had escaped. One of the Tanzanian guards was heard to marvel at the clean getaway: "They could even have pinched our guns as they went by!" he remarked to his colleagues. That day, after the head count, nothing more or out of the ordinary was done to us.

CHAPTER TEN

FAST BIND, FAST FIND

Torture us, rack us, condemn us, crush us;
your cruelty only proves our innocence:
That is why God suffers us to suffer all this.

Tertullian

THE SUDDEN AND UNEXPECTED appearance of some top brass army officers in our field the following day early in the morning augured big trouble for us. As they loitered, one of them was speaking into a walkie-talkie, so I reckoned they must have codenamed the event "Operation So and So". As we curiously and anxiously focused our attention on them through the windows of our wards, we were soon overawed by a seemingly endless parade of warders marching inside in three columns. Then they were quickly mustered, given a quick briefing and dispersed in the military manner and haste to effect surprise.

Soon they were charging towards the wards simultaneously, in contingents of about ten to each ward. All told, they must have comprised the whole body of Luzira Prison warders, at least 300 men, as far as I could guess. Thereby, we already knew their objective, so we waited for their arrival with resignation.

They were soon bearing down on us like a pack of hounds. Now wielding batons and issuing harsh orders, they harassed us out of the ward onto the court, where two of them herded us while the others proceeded to scour our house. After searching inside the ward, they searched outside too: on the rooftops, in the roof gutters; in the filthy, clogged drainage trenches they felt around for and extracted any solid substance; they looked under the inspection covers of the plumbing system—even the cesspools—and this time discovered the caches of *enguli*. All the liquor was spilled, alas, and the containers were confiscated.

In the meantime the two warders left in charge of us also frisked our persons, expecting to find a lot of money, but to no avail except for negligible small change. At the end of their search, their catch, all told, was a huge heap of all sorts of goods and chattels: every kind of furniture spared in the previous searches, iron rods, sisal mats, mattresses (naked sponge mattresses only, however, were later to be restored to their owners), all feminine wear, handbags, briefcases, belts and bottles such as might provide Molotov cocktails; all the remnant army clothes and boots were confiscated; nearly all the businessmen's wares were seized; ditto for all personal cooking pans and other utilities. In short, they took the whole kit and caboodle of what could be used in a riot or as an aid to escaping, save our personal clothes, shoes, blankets, bed sheets, soap and prison issue utensils. Even our personal cutlery was confiscated.

We had all expected stern measures to be taken in consequence of the escape, and some warders had hinted at the prospect of a rigorous search as the first step in that action. So, the evening before the search, everyone prepared for whatever was to come, rather frantically: Money and vendors' wares were hidden in gutters, in drainage trenches, under inspection covers; money was inserted between overlapping iron sheets in the roof; more was hidden in fuse boxes and in wall fissures.

In fact, we had underestimated the probing skills or the "houndmanship" of a prison warder. We were disappointed to find most of our money gone! The total loss of cash in this search must have been a staggering, six-figure fortune. One of the searchers alone was said to have stumbled upon a wad amounting to a cool 20,000 shillings!

Well, if the storekeeper (who also participated in that operation) was the lucky man, he should have amply requited the second theft of his tyres, but even if he was not the one, he must have got a share from the rest of the spoils. After the ransacking, we retrieved whatever had been spared in it; we tidied up our jumbled bedding and clothes, scattered sandals, utensils and other oddments. We were filled with a new, daunting presentiment.

As if that search was not enough, early the next morning we were again brought awake for yet another search, this time by the Tanzanian guards. While we waited out in the court, they too rummaged through our things, scattering them here and there, but they found nothing offensive nor of value. Instead they went away with the harmless and worthless paper boxes in which some inmates used to stow their clothes and other things.

Then, coming out to us, they lined us up in two rows. They first frisked everyone, and then ordered us to remove our shirts. More commands followed, which we obeyed meekly: "Open your mouths... Raise your hands high... Raise your feet..." If you had shoes or sandals on, you would have to submit them for close scrutiny. If you kept a thick thatch on your head, it would be felt lest something should be inserted there.

More orders followed:

"Drop your pants... Raise your scrotum..."

I suppose they had a terrible loathing to look in the ass because after that we were allowed to hitch up our pants back into position. Their search was over and they left penniless, for they really had no clue where to look for money. But later on, some inmates lamented the loss of their money inserted between the layers of the cardboard of the innocent paper boxes, none of which the Tanzanians spared in any ward. That money was never likely to be discovered by anyone.

In scarcely a week, another search took place by about a dozen warders. This time they were accompanied by a horde of regular jailbirds (with clean-shaven scalps) to aid them. They proved even better in snooping and probing, on the basis of send a thief to catch a thief, I suppose. By the end of their search, they had uncovered just about all our remnant dry rations, for these famished ruffians had an incentive, as they were allowed to use anything edible on the spot. Indeed they wolfed down all our canned foods while we looked on helplessly; and they went away grinning with gratification for the rare delicacies they had so enjoyed in prison. Had they but been ruminants, they could have taken leave of the stodgy prison food for several days. But so tame and subdued had we become that even such scum of the earth were placed above us in the pecking order!

This upheaval indeed made us expect to meet with harder times ahead. We feared that such shakedowns would in the long run deprive us of all our money and other personal effects if we continued to cling to them. Therefore some prisoners were now constrained to surrender to the official custody of the reception clerk their money and other valuables that had at first been ignored or had somehow eluded the searches, such as radios, watches and even their spare clothes; for it was rumoured that the searches might eventually encroach on our personal clothing too. Even still, some prisoners, against their better judgement, entrusted their savings to their so-called friendly warders or those who used to ply trade with them. There could be little surprise that their money would never be restored to them when they demanded it, eventually, because their partners, with business thus strangled, had nothing more to keep them in bond; and so thenceforth they kept out of sight of their creditors.

One such conman was the fat executioner, who was said to have walked out on his partners with an aggregate of no less than 10,000 shillings. In desperation, some prisoners had to entrust their money even to such a man as that irresponsible greedy public servant, who had so unscrupulously sold his honour for "30 silver pieces" (in the service of the Crown) by supplying contraband liquor to the prisoners, which was not only immoral but criminal!

I recall with amusement, too, that in one of the evenings following the searches, some Tanzanian guards brought in some commodities to sell; and some of our impetuous businessmen, so confident that all was now back to normal, eagerly thronged around as they were wont to do before, to buy their commodities. When the winners of the bid had paid for the goods, they were, to their dismay, not allowed to have them. Instead they were challenged to explain how come they still had money, which was offence enough? The two Tanzanians went on hawking their goods from ward-to-ward and, in the same manner, extorted more and more money from our unwary businessmen till eventually they went back with their goods "unsold"!

Soon after those searches, the abridgment of our liberty had also begun to take place piecemeal: We were no longer permitted to be anywhere in the main quad at any time unless invited there. The area around the gate was, as it were, taboo, so, naturally, the veranda tenants had to be evicted and allocated to wards. Gone were the days when we dared to reject overcrowding.

As a result, business was stifled or frustrated a great deal, for contact between prisoners of different wards was also restricted to a great extent. Even our meals were now served and eaten in the courts and no longer in the common main quad. The only opportunity to mix with prisoners from other wards was on Sunday during the religious services. I need not say that our outdoor sports would hardly ever take place again; even the French language courses had to stop before we could even speak or understand a smattering of it; only one exceptionally fast learner, however, could speak it at best after a fashion. The only vestige of trade was the furtive retail of cigarettes, which some enterprising warders still continued to supply on the sly to some mutually enterprising prisoners.

We were now left languishing within just the small spaces of the wing courts, to which there were generally three wards each in such a confined space, generally 200 inmates crowded to bask in the sun with scarcely any length to take a stroll or do any other kind of exercise. My own wanderlust was thus curbed as if on a leash!

Before long, this transition also introduced the customary routine of three lock-ups (prison jargon for head counts) daily: on waking up in the early morning, at mid-day, and in the evening before bedtime. Three pesky blasts of a whistle regularly signalled the time for a lock-up, and in a trice we would all assemble in the main quad in our ward groups, to be counted. On the first day that the warders implemented this new order, we were assembled accordingly and made to squat in two serried ranks facing each other. Two warders counted us to be doubly sure no mistake was made. A sergeant, as is the practice, was on hand to receive their simultaneous reports. One reported 66 and the other, 69.

"Do it again," snapped the sergeant irately. Blushing with chagrin, the two warders repeated their count and returned un-matching reports again! At last we could not help laughing because we knew none of them was right this time. Then the sergeant, so exasperated, took over the humble role himself and found the number to be 66, which the ward leader verified.

Even thereafter, we realised that some of the warders often found difficulties in enumerating us even when they were sober; and, to our amusement, nearly all of them were less often sober! As a result, very often too, the grand total of the prisoners was found to mismatch (without any other cause) the current lock-up figures. There were several occasions when the lock-up had to be repeated three times, and on one occasion even four times, before the correct grand total was found.

"What some of those warders deserve," quoth Colonel Mambo, "is more 'rithmetic drills."

Then followed a spell of the nastiest and most unforgettable experience of our Gethsemane, when a new brand of tyranny was unleashed upon us by two newly-come Tanzanian guards. These two guys really brought the whole prison to cringe under their inordinate ruthlessness. Even the warders themselves appeared to be so intimidated by them that they could never dare take issue with their brutal handling of the prisoners. And for several weeks neither would the superintendent lift a finger to protect us from such gratuitous cruelty, until at the last they were withdrawn from the detail:

One of the twain, probably a Maasai savage, was too gangly for a soldier; but, admittedly, even the mere sound of his gruff stentorian voice always struck terror into the hearts of quite a few of us. The companion was his opposite, being short and stocky, but his match, being equally sadistic, a fact that should have enhanced the grounds for their companionship.

They always haunted the prison together whenever they wished to brutalise the prisoners, especially whenever they had charged themselves with liquor. On the first day of their appearance, the short one entered our ward but nobody cared to acknowledge his presence. So he barked menacingly, "Prisoners, you don't stand up when I come in, eh? Alright, lie down everyone."

Before most of us had moved a muscle, he was lashing the tardy inmates and soon had us all prostrated, grovellingly, not daring to raise heads or eyes.

In the dead silence he thundered again, "Stand up everyone and line up here." We all stood up at the drop of a hat and huddled ourselves together, unsure how he wanted us lined up.

Again he lashed out with his cane in a wild rampage and soon had all of us lined up in two neat serried rows across the length of the room.

He stood in front of us menacingly and said, "Now if you have anything in your pocket, dig it out and throw it down here before I start searching. I'll have no mercy on whomever I find money on his person." Surely the bluff drove home. Out of fear of further torture and humiliation, we surrendered a small fortune to the SOB. Like a robber in a holdup, he picked up the money and scrammed.

Later we learnt that he had been to several other wards and similarly extorted more money from the inmates there. At the kitchen he heisted from the cooks, who naturally kept the biggest nest eggs, about 4,000 shillings, although he met with opposition there from The Chieftain, who, uncowed, defied him and would not submit to his solo search even though he brandished his cane at him; for The Chieftain was certain he had no orders at all from above to search the prisoners all by himself.

In another ward, this insatiable extorter had the prisoners lined up outside their ward and then demanded money from everyone in turn before letting them go inside. Anyone who did not have the smallest amount of money to give him was instead dealt a hard thrashing and warned that he had better have some money next time round.

During the head counts these tyrants would not brook any dawdling and almost always lurked nearby to spur the prisoners out of or into their wards, as the case required, using long whips. This always caused the prisoners to panic and scamper in or out like goaded, frightened animals—even when these terrorist rogues were not nearby—for fear that a whip might crash on one's back if one brought up the rear. Thus some prisoners hurt themselves in the undue panic, during the stampede for the narrow doors.

The height of their insanity was unleashed upon a certain group of officers, whom they grossly humiliated in full view of their subordinate ranks, who were duly appalled: After the head count, the officers were dismissed with a vicious crack of the whip, which struck some of them at the rear of the rows. That sent them all racing slapdash, pell-mell for the door to their ward upstairs. But at the landing the other bully too stood brandishing his whip menacingly. Now they were trapped in that bottleneck, with the retreat as formidable as the advance. Rather instinctively, they collectively chose the brunt of the advance and were soon licking their wounds in the sanctuary of their ward. Some of them sustained sprains apart from the welts of the whips.

That ordeal had been so mortifying that The Chieftain found grounds this time to complain to the superintendent, and it was not long before we breathed a sigh of relief from their nightmare.

In the meantime work had started and was being carried on daily to rehabilitate the broken or jammed locks. So far they could keep us pent-up in the wing enclaves only. Now it was evident their purpose was to have us eventually locked up inside the wards. They could not, however, repair or even replace the locks of the tiny individual cells, whose solid doors of a rare type of hardwood had built-in locks of some special, but outmoded construction. For the past few days some prison officers had been reconnoitring the locks of the main doors and had found a solution in consequence:

Some public works carpenters were assigned to undertake the repairs and were always overseen at work by at least one prison officer plus several warders, presumably to make sure no monkey tricks could be played by the repairman. In his professional judgment, if the carpenter deemed a lock was improper or insufficient for this or that door, he would suggest, say, a chain instead; and sure enough a monstrous chain, such as only the legendary Hercules might undo, would be installed. From then on we would be haunted by the harsh sound of the clank of steel chains upon steel doors, a sound at first so unearthly to our ears and so perturbing, but a sound we had yet to become accustomed to. Until I find use for them, I hate carpenters. First they nailed my Lord Jesus Christ, and now they had me nailed in also!

Before the carpenters had completed the repairs of all the locks and before the warders could start locking up the prisoners inside the wards, two youths escaped by scaling the wall somehow. In the process they wound their way over the roof-top of The Chieftain's upstairs ward at the north-eastern corner. The Chieftain, who heard the sound of their movement, called out to them to come back but they merely snarled back at him, "Who are you to us?"

The Chieftain himself reported the escape, which at that very instant brought the warders and the Tanzanians swarming all over the place. They went to every ward and harshly brought inmates awake for head counts. In the ward from where the youths escaped, the inmates were flogged in merciless wrath. The next day or so, the repairs on the locks were expedited, and for the first time we were bolted in for the night, and for the rest of the term we were to be so treated.

Some wards had their toilets out in the courts, so the inmates had to make do with buckets to pee and defecate in at night. The most unabashed disregard for privacy was witnessed: Whenever a man had the runs too, he would make several trips to the common chamber pot (placed at one end of the room) to relieve himself with a horrible thunder and stench in the glare of the other inmates, who had to choke as they masked their snouts in trying not to sniff the revolting stench.

Now was the time that the plastic sanitary pails were badly missed. Just one of these things, however, had been spared from the wanton destruction of the tea-and-toast merchants, and indeed, by a funny happening, it had remained in the sole possession of a fat cook, who was known to shit more by night than by day, for every morning, he was seen slopping out into a toilet. So the inmates humorously tagged him *Mtu ya* Briefcase, otherwise Briefcase Man. Anyway, I found out then why prisoners smell so disgustingly different: because some of them sleep with their dung!

The congestion was now felt more than ever before. We could no longer go to the communal showers; instead the buckets we peed in were the very containers out of which we bathed and in which we washed our clothes. There were always too many people waiting for their turn to use them, few as they were.

Early morning entailed long processions to the toilets, and because the warders waited impatiently to lock-up the prisoners inside the wards again, they had to relieve themselves in haste and maybe only in part. Yet, even in such circumstances, I note, some Muslims of a fundamentalist cult would nonetheless be obliged to do their ritual ablutions in the toilets: You could always see some of them with plastic flasks of all sorts in the queues! In their turns, however, they usually took up an unreasonably long time, much to the annoyance of others in the queue. Nay, such ablutions were also unsavoury to think of especially whenever soap was in short supply.

It was sometimes the arbitrary whim of some warders to give us extra hours in the sun or deny us what the prison regulations concede for exercise. The Tanzanians also seemed to have prevailed upon the prison authorities to keep us under lock and key during rain. From the escape of the seven men in the rain, the Tanzanians coined another proverb: "Prisoners use rain as a vehicle to escape". So, whenever there was rain or if the sky was gestating it all day long, that would mean a day in hibernation. Indeed, an opportunity for prisoners to be outside their wards during the day is, to a certain extent, a risk.

Prisoners do escape somehow even in broad daylight! Now and then, the harsh blast of the dreary siren, which might buzz continuously for about a quarter-of-an-hour, tolls the escape of another prisoner from any of the penitentiaries during the day. Whenever this happens, all the prisoners in all the four penitentiaries making up Luzira Prison are required to be under a curfew or under lock and key until the issue is closed.

Pent-up in wards or in courts nearly all day, the prisoners were left with scarcely any opportunity to air their bedding in the sun; therefore the lice increased and multiplied again into myriads. The old squalor and bad hygiene were inevitable. Waste food and other filth were dumped carelessly within the courts because the prisoners seldom found time and chance to toss them out into the proper receptacles. Bathing, washing clothes, washing utensils and brushing teeth were all done within the courts. Such conditions indeed attracted swarms of flies.

In this new regime of confinement, prisoners would not be allowed to go outside their court unescorted. Even fetching water from the hydrants at the main quad called for an escort. And the number of prisoners in need of medical treatment had to be arbitrarily (and rather artificially) regulated because it became apparent that most prisoners wanted to avail themselves of an opportunity merely to take a leisurely stroll under the essential sunshine, or visit friends at Soweto, or in quest of the latest news there (for Soweto was reputed to be the cradle of all rumour), and not least, to ogle the hospital employees. Thus there was always a fabulous number of sick prisoners.

So the regulations allotted days of the week and times of day to specific wards to visit the hospital, which meant that if a man was sick, he would have only to wait until the day and time his ward was slated to visit the hospital. (But still, in this case, those who were not sick would nevertheless seize the opportunity to go out to the hospital.) A serious case that warranted admission, however, would be considered regardless of the regulation concerned. In that case the sick man would have to be borne by other prisoners to emphasise the gravity of his illness, even if the sick man could actually get there under his own steam. Thereby the willing bearers, usually some half-a-dozen of them, also found an opportunity to go to Soweto for medicine or for any other purpose.

Prisoners sometimes used this as a way out or *madaraka*, as soldiers call it, meaning "tricks", to get a ticket to Soweto and to the hospital: A man would pretend to swoon or would feign serious illness; his friends would call round a warder to see him in that state. Then the warder would understandingly certify him as deserving medical attention with no delay, and would let some half-a-dozen of them assist the "sick" man to the hospital.

As a result of these changes too, there was now much work and much ado for the prison keepers. Newly-passed-out warders were engaged and posted to oversee all the gateways to the various wings. Even the Tanzanian guards were reinforced by our own new UNLA recruits, which intensified our misgivings and creepiness even more, for we generally thought they were apt to have bad blood against us and therefore likely to be more ruthless than the Tanzanians were; and at first they appeared to be too arrogant and aloof to approach any prisoner. Our suspicions and fears, however, were soon allayed by the national prejudice that prevailed in our favour, for they soon discovered amongst us their own kith and kin, instead of the fabulous Sudanese Foreign Legion that Amin was said to have left behind.

But all these sudden and sweeping changes at Upper Prison had not been merely the result of the seven escaped prisoners. The moves must have been contemplated even earlier as a security precaution for the forthcoming elections, and that escape merely precipitated them being put into force.

Back on the 27th of May 1980, following immediately after the removal of Binaisa and the subsequent assumption of power by the Military Commission, Obote made his historic return home after nine years of exile in Tanzania. But Obote, while still in Dar es Salaam even after the exit of Amin, had appeared to be silent and aloof from the affairs of Uganda to make believe he was not laying claim to his past status as the president of Uganda, for it might have been generally considered that his pre-eminence in the foreground of the liberation campaign could, because of hostile prejudice against him particularly in Buganda, have jeopardised the chances of winning the war against Amin. For, indeed, Amin had always, to some measure of success, exploited the bogeyman in Obote to the Baganda. But, undoubtedly, in some other parts of the country, Obote, who possibly had the most formidable military and political power base in his sway, remained a charismatic idol. Therefore his image and the spectre of his returning to power haunted his enemies, Amin's soldiers in detention, and, nay, Binaisa was the most perturbed about it. Yet Binaisa had once been caricatured in one of the tabloids of yellow journalism and lampoonery of his time as compliantly warming-up the presidential chair for Obote! Binaisa would deny this point-blank while he was still perched on that chair.

The news of Obote's return was cause for great worry to the prisoners in particular, and more so had his come-back become disquieting when he unravelled Binaisa's intrigue. Making a great show of emotions in speeches to crowds that welcomed him back home as he barnstormed the country, Obote charged, among other things, that Binaisa, with a selfish motive, had indicated his loathing for his rightful return home from exile. Moreover, he went on, instead of according priority and due attention to the plight of the repatriated exiles and their dependants, the widows and orphans (for whom Obote showed an oversentimental concern), Binaisa, having an axe to grind, had been obsessed only with the plans for releasing from jails Amin's soldiers, "Just the very killers of yesterday back to kill innocent people again"!

On hearing such a view, some of the prisoners were deprived of their appetites for several days, for they concluded at once that the underlying meaning could only be that Amin's soldiers should never be released at all. So was the suspicion given substance that, well behind the scenes, Obote, Nyerere's long-time protégé, while still in Dar es Salaam, must have, after all, been manipulating the puppet strings to keep Amin's soldiers purposefully pent-up in prison. That was likely why Binaisa's initiatives to release them had always been overruled by the Tanzanian supreme authority in Kampala.

As far as some prisoners were concerned, Obote, compared with Amin, was only just the lesser devil. If he came to power, therefore, indefinite detention could be our lot to say the least, or so it was generally feared. Although Obote's later campaign gambits were conciliatory and hinting at clemency for the prisoners (so were the other three candidates in the presidential race), many prisoners would remain unsettled nonetheless, as they could not trust those "catch-vote" gimmicks. It was commonly known that Obote had a reputation for a forked tongue and a record tarnished with indefinite unlawful detentions under the pretext of a state of emergency. And what if he was harbouring a passion for revenge?

It is not improbable either that some of Obote's antagonists and detractors, wishing to discredit him the more, played on such bad prejudice against him to sow seeds of rebellion and foment further unrest in the prisoners by spreading the theory that Obote was hell-bent on wreaking revenge on Amin's soldiers; and some of the tale-bearing visitors to Upper Prison might have been the unwitting agitators. The postponement of the elections and the recent ban on visitors mounted further disquiet and the suspicion that worse was yet to come.

Such fear was abroad in the prison. It led to the escape of the seven men against all the odds. Moreover, some prisoners earlier, as the polling day was drawing closer, had carelessly given vent to their sentiments, saying that they would have no other choice but to break out of jail in the event that Obote bounced back to power; the stool-pigeons in our midst must have done their duty, of course. Consequently, the escape of the seven men must have corroborated the dangerous atmosphere reigning over Upper Prison and brought the military officers around to forestall, as it were, a possible mutiny or even a prison break. Besides, where would an escaped prisoner go? In all probability he would go underground, which would be in bad taste to the Government. Hadn't they after all learnt the lesson practically that he who fights and runs away, may live to fight another day? And isn't there a vernacular saying that "a runaway prisoner has swallowed an axe!"

Following that escape, one of the commanders of the city garrisons was deputed to give a dressing-down to the prisoners. So that high and mighty officer harangued us with a barrage of rhetorical questions:

"Why do you want to escape?"

"Where do you want to go, to exile?"

"To do what?...To become guerrillas?"

"Do you think life in exile is sweet?...And if you want to become guerrillas, do you think life in the bush is a bed of roses?"

"Do you think the people you want to fight are not armed and ready to fight back too?"

"Listen, when we were in exile we had to clear jungles and till the earth. Believe me, we had to toil daily with sweat in order to subsist. Here in prison you live so comfortably; you eat without toil; you sleep in good houses; you have electricity and running water, none of the amenities we knew during all our eight years of exile. *So why escape?*"

He took a pause to let his points sink home, and then continued, "Now is our turn to rule the roost, therefore, you people had better be patient here and wait for yours. But if you weary of life here, simply take a rope and hang. But you needn't even try that because I am sure there will always be plenty of people around to rescue you...".

Then, in a tame tone, almost conciliatory, he went on to say that it behoved us only to be patient till things sorted themselves out; that the trouble really was that "everybody wants to be the President of Uganda", that a Muganda was "so tribal-centred and thinks he is more Ugandan than others. Is it because the name Uganda derives from Buganda?" he wondered; that Lule, who had been in an exile of all beer and skittles, had been installed as the president of the caretaker Government by virtue of a show of hands by only a handful of exiles in Moshi, but no sooner had they settled back home than he had wanted to force some of them back into exile.

Then they had peacefully replaced him with Binaisa, another Muganda, who had also been handed the presidency by another handful of members of an electoral college; that it was Binaisa who, for selfish purposes, had tried to unleash Amin's soldiers from jail, only with an aim to dislodge some of them who had actually offered their blood, toil and sweat to eject Amin. Therefore, they had found cause to depose that armchair liberator too, who had only flown from America with a briefcase; that they had done so in the national interest, as they were doing their best to preclude the menace and danger of another catastrophe that could be caused by power-hungry scramblers; that they hoped to achieve this by letting them contest matters with the country-wide ballot instead of with the bullet; that Paulo Muwanga (then chairman of the incumbent Military Commission, and to all intents and purposes the President of Uganda during this interregnum, who did not even care to veil his bias in favour of UPC, Obote's party) was the only good Muganda left, in whom they still placed their trust for their cherished goal, which was to lead the people of Uganda to "free and fair elections…".

At the end of his philippic, he departed with a promise that he would in future be paying us monthly visits for more of his lectures. That was the note that worried us all the more, because it seemed to carry a subtext that (at best) we still had a long, long way to go here, or that (at worst) we had been institutionalised.

Yet, on the eve of the elections, we witnessed, unbelievingly, the departure of two high-ranking officers. This took place in the bright morning, and the scene was dramatised with dancing for joy (as though the two men had just won a sweepstake) and falling on their knees to pray and pay thanks, loudly chanting some doxology to Allah, as the doors were about to yield to them.

A scandalous rumour later claimed that those officers, reputedly men of untold substance, had won their freedom not entirely from Allah but had been redeemed upon payment of heavy ransoms to the Tanzanian army chiefs. Could the very votaries of the socialist creed and virtues so compromise their reputation with bribes? One of the two men, the object of so much sensation and disbelief, was a former provost marshal (commander of the terrorist military police), of whom there was cause to believe he would leave prison last if ever he would, or else he was a cinch for the "necktie", for his wickedness during his tenure was generally considered unpardonable. This incident certainly gave rise to a new, though seemingly absurd fear that future releases would be influenced and secured with nothing else than money, and that the highest bidders would be the better off: survival of the richest, that is.

The long-awaited polling day at last came, and our own anxiety about that crucial event was obvious, for we still trusted that our very salvation could come with another change in political leadership. As freedom of expression had been throttled by the recent upheaval and tension, the prisoners could only silently will the DP to win the elections. So, when at first a rumour pervaded that it had done so, most of us, confident that the election result was cut and dried, could not help showing our elation, and as we waited anxiously and tensely for the official confirmation, there were already naïve hopes and new reassurances of going home the following day or the following week.

Our hopes were soon dashed by the controversial radio statement that the UPC had won. (This controversial verdict would become the grievance and the cause of — or was it the excuse for? — more rebel movements, which claimed that Obote had rigged the elections or that the results of the elections had been falsified or doctored.) For our part, generally speaking, there were expressions of disapproval and signs of despondency everywhere, as state power had thus rotated back to Obote. The days to follow were the most dismal, in a state of complete uncertainty.

Christmas, our second in prison, was at hand. Our Red Cross patrons, like Santa Claus, brought us their timely gifts, namely biscuits, sugar and milk-powder. Hot water was available from the kitchen to enable everyone to have "high tea" during Christmas; the services were attended as zealously as ever by most of our predominantly Christian community.

Sometime in January 1981, our hopes were rekindled when the newly-installed president announced, for the first time, his intention to release prisoners. Although the announcement was rather vague, it was taken to be definite or even definitive. So the pent-up rumours were reborn and circulated as usual, naming the date of departure but always missing the target — and then setting a new one again.

· · · · · · · · · · · · · · · · · ·

ABOUT A MONTH ELAPSED after that announcement and the prisoners lost faith in it; the rumours about departure could no longer be taken so seriously. It seemed the president had gone back on his word. Little wonder two sub-alterns made their escape, using water pipes, electric conduits and gutters to aid them to the roof-top of their ward at the north-eastern corner. Once on the roof, they made a derring-do free-fall down the two storeys. That must have taken the pluck of a most desperate man, or a stunt man! The escape was discovered early in the morning and there was much ado as usual, as well as, of course, the flogging of the ward mates of the escaped prisoners.

The puzzle of this escape was explained thus: Although the prisoners were locked inside the ward, these two escapees did not have to force open any door. All head counts were then conducted outside the wards; that particular evening, however, before locking up for the night, the two prisoners had availed themselves of an opportunity to sneak inside the outside toilets of their ward as the other ward mates were entering it for the night. The warder who had just counted them, completely unaware of their sneak action, locked them out. The two men waited for the best hour of night to make their escape. That oversight had to be corrected at once and so, to close the last loophole, or so they thought, the warders started conducting head counts inside the wards before locking up for the night.

While we still pinned some hopes on the last presidential pronouncement, a sudden anti-climax killed them altogether. I cannot for the life of me recall the exact date but it must have been a night in mid-February. The hour was long past midnight. A single thunder-like blast from a blockbuster smote the still night and brought us instantly awake. Similar explosions followed in rapid succession, then a chorus of rifle fire chimed in to make a formidable drumfire, whose projectiles seemed to be passing over our roof or falling near our walls.

We shook and fumbled in utter panic: There was a loud clanging of pans and plates kicked about in the dark as we sleepily scrambled to our feet. We groped our way, bumping into one another. There was a pandemonium of panic-stricken voices, and someone shouted above it all, "Switch on the lights!" Instantly the lights came on.

The room was in a shambles: In the confusion the floor had been strewn with the leftover *ugali*, pans, mugs, bowls, blankets and so forth. A naked man was still trying with difficulty to get into his pants, first mixing up the trouser legs, and then starting all over again. The fright had made some others involuntarily piss in their pants. In a helter-skelter some inmates were already making a surge for the door, purporting to force it open. I vaguely recall that only the ward leader seemed to keep calm and it was he who announced to us firmly and reproachfully that it was far more hopeless to panic; where could we run to, after all? By so panicking, we could easily compound the danger, so it was far better we stayed calm, he cautioned.

The would-be door busters thought better of it. We all ceased our Bedlam and became placable, but our hearts still raced at a rapid pace, with a silent prayer, as gunfire raged on unabated for a gruelling, long hour or so. There was not a moment's peace of mind: If this incident had taken place in the days before we went under lock and key, you can imagine the magnitude of the chaos and disaster that could have attended.

The big guns had long fallen silent and by the crack of dawn the noise had abated to sporadic single bursts of rifle fire; and at that time a certain warder sneaked around and spoke to us, as anxious as we were, from an open window, but he was as ignorant of the situation as we were because, said he, nobody was allowed to enter or leave the prison.

In the blessed silence and calm that followed this storm, the rest of the day still appeared to be fraught with danger. Hardly anybody could be seen moving about the place; it seemed all our prison keepers had deserted the prison.

It was not until about five o'clock in the afternoon that we were let out into the court at last, and with such anxiety we learnt the first unofficial news that the pre-dawn skirmish had been an attempt by some anti-Government dissidents to spring the prisoners from jail. By another contradictory account, it was a stage-managed battle to frame a spurious charge of treason or mutiny against the prisoners so as to justify their long confinement.

Another jolly sergeant-major explained the conflict with this imagery: "At Upper Prison is a most desirable coquette. She flirts about and provokes jealousy in her rival lovers, who are eventually drawn to a duel to win her," he said, adding, "If the dissidents want us, the Government want us no less — for good or for bad."

I was also to gather later that some inmates could have been in cahoots with the rebels but only a very few of the most trusted might have been privy to the rescue plan. In any case, it looked as though the event had irremediably foiled our chances of release.

I need hardly say that night we went hungry too. Of absolute necessity our cooks had to stay away from the kitchen during the whole day of tension.

CHAPTER ELEVEN

LATTER DAYS

Unearned suffering is redemptive.

Martin Luther King, Jr

THE FOLLOWING DAY WE learnt that outside the prison there was much ado and sensation about the incident and a general fear that Upper Prison and its malcontents had been wiped out in what was believed to have been a tragic hecatomb. Although the rescue attempt had been a fiasco, reinforcements had pitched camp around the whole prison and were dwelling in foxholes.

The prison warders themselves were no longer trusted and were always searched on entry and exit. It turned out that some of them were suspected of complicity in the abortive rescue and were arrested. The hospital sister and her assistant could no longer bear the situation and they eventually stopped reporting for duty because of the humiliating and immodest search they had to routinely submit to on entry and exit. The hospital, thence, had to be run by a certain warder and a number of our own medical orderlies.

We ourselves felt the screw tightened further. Possession of money was an offence; but now, moreover, possession of any kind of documents — even legitimate identity papers, old letters and any other stationery items — was regarded as unlawful. Those who kept diaries had to flush them down a toilet. Random searches were carried out almost daily as the inmates sought desperately for new hiding places: Money was skilfully waxed in soap or inserted in used-up toothpaste tubes, in the leftover *ugali*, in the spines of some old-world books issued by the prison library, now the only documents allowed in the prisoners' possession. Another method, though rare, was to sandwich the money in the split sole of a sandal or shoe and sew it in.

The random searches were now assigned to and carried out by two particular warders who were notorious for their robot-like lack of human feeling and understanding. Both of them were tall and lean, showing mean and hungry looks; and because of their overbearing position over us they always displayed a false sense of pride and satisfaction with their job, which we could not help scoffing and sneering at (of course behind their backs or in our secret thoughts). These two were as despicable and odious as the tax collectors, or even more so because the money they always seized from the prisoners they would never be obliged to hand in to the national exchequer for the common good. That incentive indeed explained why their quest for money was so painstakingly thorough that it would at times go as far as inspecting the prisoners' fundaments or ordering them to squat so that the money could obey the law of gravity.

But one day, certain inmates tricked one of them into taking along with him a lump of human excrement instead: They wrapped the faeces with the old disused currency notes, which bore Amin's long-forgotten, dreaded effigy. Then they bound the whole bundle with cellophane to make believe it was a huge bankroll (The currency notes that had just come into circulation were replicas of the old notes but minus Amin's portrait.) They then "hid" this bundle where it could be discovered. The hound did, and rapaciously pocketed it. The inmates never had a heartier laugh!

Some inmates had also found another way of hoodwinking them: Even before they were told what to do, they would drop down their pants and shoot their hands high up with complete abandon in readiness for the search, as if to say, "Alright, search us if you think we have anything to hide." The searcher, seeing their ready submission and their ingratiating manner, would understandably be disarmed and, believing there was really nothing to search and bother them for, would either ignore them or frisk them cursorily. In that way those inmates always got away with their money, skilfully sandwiched between their fingers or their toes, and under their ear lobes, amused at the success of their ruse.

These two hounds one day pounced on the hospital, that inviolate institution, which had always been exempted from searches, and ransacked it through and through, scaring and worrying the bedridden patients. Their quarry this time was a little portable radio, the presence of which they had learnt about from their treacherous informers.

Somewhere at the hospital used to be the hide-out for this radio, and some inmates used to secrete themselves there to listen to news. Counter-informers had also given their timely warning about the planned raid on the hospital. The owner of the radio spirited it away pronto. Wherever the new hiding and listening post was, the hounds could never after all their efforts discover it. The inmates continued to be fed with radio broadcasts (including the BBC News) from this source. Moreover, in spite of this intense restraint, some prisoners were nonetheless still able to smuggle in and out uncensored letters, oral messages and even money by suborning some warders, who became their constant couriers.

Meanwhile, the battle over Upper Prison had given our pessimists and worriers grounds to believe that Obote had actually come back to exact his pound of flesh and was now exhorting, "Jailer, look to them…"

Few could now dispel the possibility of getting killed in prison. Our safety was now in great doubt; even Obote's adherents in the prison (some of whom had arrogated to themselves the duty to spy and snitch on fellow prisoners, thereby hoping to curry favours) could no longer help entertaining the fears that we, as a whole, were expendable. And even if our lives were to be spared after all, there was no longer any guarantee that we would leave prison soon.

As one minister had once berated us, we had been the "tools of a murderous reign". The allegory of the "tools" may best explain our new situation: The workman need never take out his tools unless there was work to be done with them. But then he had acquired a new set of tools in spite of the old ones. If he disposed of the old ones from the store, another rival workman would surely lay claim to them and he would be jealous of that too. In that case, then, would the workman discharge the old tools from the store or might not he as well say, "Well, let them gather rust in the store till they become absolutely disused"? The fear of the latter could become a reality: The spectre of being condemned to stay in prison indefinitely was the most haunting and excruciating. In my heart of hearts, it would be better to be dead than continue to exist here!

Meanwhile too, anxiety was clearly expressed by the prisoners that they might be suspected of complicity one way or another in the attempt to spring them. Therefore, a succinct note to protest our innocence was written to the president and endorsed by the superintendent. Its contents—I got no opportunity to copy them verbatim—have long eluded my memory, but in sum and substance it begged to dissociate the prisoners from any treasonous activities whatever, with particular reference to the recent pre-dawn armed conflict over our prison.

Meanwhile too, our restraint was intensified further yet, conceding us even less time still in the open. Our food was now served and eaten inside the wards and no longer out in the courts. The predominantly indoor life added yet new elements of ennui. Now with the prospects of regaining our freedom seemingly in jeopardy, we felt robbed of the purpose and gusto to simply be, which made most of us lethargic and emasculated. With hardly room or opportunity for locomotion, we felt sitting fatigue, pins and needles. Games of cards and checkers were now left as the only animation and soul of our passive and suspenseful existence. I once read from some book (I can't call it to mind) that freedom, until lost, is never appreciated. Now I would fully subscribe to that observation. Imagine, we were pining for our former liberty and privileges, appreciating the escapades of our good old salad days! The freedom beyond seemed as remote as another planet—a mirage!

Fortunately, however, our Red Cross patrons soon came up with another kind of remedy for our passivity and ennui. This time they donated several hundred books to offer us wide and interesting reading. Thus the scanty prison library of the past-generation, of dust-ridden hardbacks, was given its biggest boost ever. To a bibliophile like me, the best-sellers among them particularly presented a delectable feast! From then on, nearly every one of us became a bookworm or simply kept a novel without ever reading it at all. Colonel Mambo once observed, not without amusement, that The Chieftain (who was not infrequently the butt of his jokes) once borrowed an English novel and returned it after only two days, the same book that he himself (Mambo) had earlier taken a whole week to read; yet The Chieftain, his cellmate, spent all the morning in kitchen administration and all the afternoon napping or, as Colonel Mambo used to say jestingly of him, "lying in state."

Some inmates committed a lot of mayhem on some of these paperbacks by using them in place of toilet tissue. So it was sometimes disappointing to find a good novel with several middle pages torn out!

By now the old famine had found its way in again, with the yellow maize donation depleted. Deprived of our visitors' supplements, the tea-and-toast retail business, and having no other source of food, we were left high and dry and had to rely on just the prison provisions, which unfortunately had also declined from three meals back to the old *modus vivendi* of one meal at sunset. As it never rains but it pours, other misfortunes befell us: The electric boilers were breaking down more often than ever; and the gas kitchen was seldom refuelled, so that we had to resort again to the laborious and time-consuming burning of firewood, which was still as hard to obtain as ever.

As another security measure now required that prisoners be in bed by seven pm, it meant going to bed without food at all if the flour and beans arrived late in the afternoon and the cooks could not cope with that time constraint. Even seven pm as bedtime was said to be leniently extended to accommodate our unique circumstances, otherwise the normal regulation bedtime is abridged to four pm. We can be sure that prisoners would have no complaint about the time allotted for sleep, but the problem is how to sleep all those long hours!

Lack of transport and lack of fuel at times were still abiding problems to make us go without food at least several times more. So most of the prisoners had to resort again to the severe measure of husbanding *ugali* from one sunset to the next to forestall the probable lack of it the following day. In other words, they would eat the previous day's food in order to sustain the new helping for the following sunset.

The other causes of food shortages were of our own making. As the kitchen was now our only feeding source, the buyers of food increased again and the cooks were abetted to become more acquisitive than ever. So, once again, they had started encroaching on much more food as their bonuses, thus stinting the general portions for the rest of the prisoners. The cooks prospered all the more in this situation as they feathered their nests, kept lusty bodies, grew fatter on better and more food, and had the enviable privilege and liberty to be in the sunshine as much as they liked. They even displayed an attitude of arrogance and smugness to the rest of the inmates. In a way, they were a sort of clique and the only equals of the prison warders, with whom they shared mutual respect. How freakish that one of them, as it was heard, wondered why people were so obsessed with thoughts of going home "so soon". Coming from a cook, it could not be taken as a joke because he must have been thinking of the vested interest he would lose by that. Anyway, the cooks were envied more than ever, and for the rest of the inmates, who begrudged them their well-being and terribly resented them, there was no more source of income, and they grew poorer as they grew thinner and unhealthier on meagre rations and from the shortage of sunshine. There was a general discontent; there was so much cause for grumbling again.

The inmates of a certain ward invited The Chieftain to account for the acute shortage of food, rearing to launch a broadside at him. So The Chieftain (for he had heard that some inmates had talked of impeaching him and appointing another officer in his place) went disarmingly before the disgruntled inmates:

"Yes, I am ready to hear your grievances and take your suggestions...."

So they heckled him: How many bags of flour were apportioned daily? And with that amount of flour couldn't they really dish out larger rations than what prisoners could barely survive on?

The old man answered that the ten bags of flour apportioned each day should, in fact, provide adequate rations but the quantity had to be diminished to make up for the cooks' remuneration.

There were obstreperous contentions that that was a lame and unjustifiable excuse, until someone posed another question, "What is the total number of the kitchen workers?"

The Chieftain declared the number to be an astounding "Two hundred" amid shouts of "What! Impossible! Incredible!"

"Fire them all!" someone thundered.

And another retorted amid general laughter, "Let's start with *him*...."

When the uproar had died down, another voice demanded in disbelief, "Is all that number so necessary?"

As if to answer the question and to cut a long story short, another inmate stood up and asserted that there were actually about 40 active cooks, who, moreover, took turns taking a two-day lay-off. The rest were a redundant lot of hangers-on in the names of dishwashers, sweepers, kitchen police and even batmen of certain officers; most if not all of them had to be pruned forthwith, he declared.

The suggestion was greeted with wild acclamation, and before the hubbub stopped another inmate solicited silence and weighed in with his endorsement of that motion: "Make a drastic cut on the cooks, the sweepers and the dishwashers, but the entire kitchen police must be disbanded because they do nothing there at all; instead, their very presence at the gate facilitates contacts between the cooks and their food buyers; they have contradicted and defeated the very purpose for which they were founded. When they were deployed there, they were supposed to keep people not authorised to be there away from the kitchen and gate, but nowadays are doing the very opposite. Therefore, demobilise them and leave the gate always locked; nobody will ever have need to approach it again because the connection to the cooks will have been broken …"

That also brought down the house again.

"What about the drum-driver?" another propounded, amid laughter.

The drum-driver was a man who had the monopoly of disposing of waste from the kitchen to the common dump in a drum, which he "drove" by rotating it at a tilt with one hand at the brim, as if he were rotating a steering wheel, like it was so second nature to him that some inmates used to marvel at his unique sleight-of-hand. But he alone could not make our rations any lighter, so that the inmates concurred he could stay. (A unique case of "safety in singleness"!). All the wood cutters too were indispensable, it was agreed, unanimously.

At the end of the debate and deliberations, it was resolved to reduce the number of the kitchen staff to about 60, eliminating the entire kitchen police. The decision was taken as the consensus of the entire Upper Prison.

Those who survived the axe were cautioned not to abuse their privilege by taking more food than would be reasonable, else they too would be replaced. Thus this revolution in the kitchen restored our rations to satisfactory quantities. Forever afterwards, food complaints would not occur. For the axed kitchen workers it would be hard going adjusting to the tougher conditions they had been dodging. They would also lose weight before long, and that was another thing for the rest of the inmates to gloat over.

At last Upper Prison also lifted its transport shortage when it received three brand new British Leyland trucks to pension off its old Bedford, a lop-sided jalopy that was prone to breaking down and delaying deliveries. So, from then on, our food store was always replenished in good time. However, quoth Colonel Mambo, "They could have put those trucks to far better use smuggling coffee out of Uganda!"

Now the vestige of business, which was never to be phased out entirely, was the furtive retailing of cigarettes. Most of the smokers had little or no money left to afford the expensive cigarettes. Soon factory-made cigarettes were substituted by the cheap unrefined *taba* foils supplied by the ever enterprising bootleggers. With these dry leaves the diehard smokers made their roll-your-owns using any brand of coarse paper, and smoked them in associations that guaranteed everyone a puff even if one was not able to afford any (Still, if *taba* foils were unavailable or unaffordable, some resorted to experimenting on dry eucalyptus leaves or even tea!). A light was hard to obtain, as matches were outlawed or too expensive. Instead the smokers used razor-blades to conjure up fire: A razor-blade was scraped on the concrete floor to produce sparks. The flying sparks would be adroitly trapped on a small mass of cotton, which would come instantly aglow for lighting the primitive cigars.

The congestion in this indoor regime, as I have already said, was now more pronounced than ever. Yet, even as the new Government took over the reins of power, they continued to populate Upper Prison with their new-found political enemies, who included some UPC renegades too, and the offenders in the illicit trade, popularly known as *magendoists*, otherwise black marketeers, on whom the Government had begun to crack down. So, then, they would never draw the line anywhere at all.

At night the prisoners were deserted in an utter palsy, without provision whatever against the contingency of an Act of God, as God may not help those that do not help themselves. Once the inmates of a certain ward had to shout at the top of their lungs for dear life as a fire was smouldering somewhere, possibly caused by a faulty electric circuit. Their cries went out in vain. Thank goodness, however, somehow the fire was dowsed; but had that been an intractable blaze, those inmates, unable to run anywhere, could have been roasted alive. Likewise if an inmate were suddenly taken seriously ill at night, there would be no way of summoning help. The warders took meticulous precautions only to have the prisoners securely bolted in but never took care to be near-at-hand in case of any emergency.

The meagre and monotonous diet made us more susceptible to diseases. The congestion, abject squalor and bad hygiene created more swarms of flies and other vermin; the mouldy food that many prisoners used to save, and on which flies flitting from the clogged toilets and filthy garbage roosted all day and night, must have contributed to the incidence and spread of disease, the most prevalent symptoms being dysentery. Deficiency maladies were equally on the rise once more. The hospital was soon crowded with in-patients; and by now prisoners had died at least by the score merely because of a lack of medicine, intensive care and a deficient diet. (I particularly recall three deaths that presented us a poignant *memento mori*: One prisoner in his mid-thirties died quietly in his sleep without having complained of illness to anyone; two others in their mid-twenties took ill one moment and died the next — within hours of each other!).

Drugs had become rarer than ever simply because the Red Cross medical subsidies, even if they found their way into the prison hospital, would hardly reach the prisoners without money to buy them from the black market. Little wonder, then, that the prisoners could ill-afford to listen to the superintendent's appeal to the "healthy prisoners" to donate blood for our anaemic victims and starvelings. If mere non-prescription drugs earmarked for the prisoners could hardly reach them, unless they had money to buy them from the black market, what would happen, then, to the much more invaluable blood? Would that not be turning the other cheek as well? Anyway, the more pertinent question was, apart from the cooks, maybe, were there any healthy prisoners left?

The superintendent's next appeal was most welcome. This time he was prompted to request a thorough cleaning of the prison, which was due to be inspected by a team of high-ranking Government officials who were on a country-wide tour of prisons. He said that the visitors' fact-finding mission would take into account the condition of the prisoners in order to give a first-hand report and opinion to the president; therefore, we should look our worst to court their sympathy, he advised.

Accordingly, we made the place spick-and-span on the eve of their arrival, and we really did our best to look our worst, dressed in the shabbiest outfits on the day they arrived. The visitors, about six of them, on their tour from ward-to-ward, came and stood at our door and uttered a greeting, which we returned listlessly from where we sat by our scanty bedding. Then they stared at us for quite a while in silence. Our appearance and pose must have had terrible pathos for them, seeming like abject hopelessness. Our melting gaze at them, moreover, must have been an effective vehicle for our distress message, which they should have understood somehow, even though nothing further was uttered between them and us. Among themselves, however, they exchanged brief, inaudible consultations. Then they turned and left for other wards. If they were good ombudsmen, which we expected they would be, they should have reported their finding and opinion with due sympathy for the prisoners.

The superintendent's next announcement was the fearful news of an outbreak of typhoid fever in one of the other penitentiaries. To avert the evil, therefore, he gave us a lecture on the health code to be observed. We all co-operated anxiously. But, surely, divine intervention must have always played a greater part to avert the potential outbreak of epidemics in such highly-charged conditions as ours, without any preventive measures whatever; as the saying goes: "God tempers the wind to the shorn lamb".

The *Bazungu* were our next visitors, a short while after their last appearance. On this visit they brought us more soap and some hand-me-down clothes. The trousers and the shirts could not go around all the prisoners, so, in doling them out, special consideration was given to the most seedily dressed prisoners. The *Bazungu* also donated to us a lot of ghee, and for the first time and until our departure from prison, our sauce was always seasoned with that savoury, dairy-flavoured, nourishing substance. Our meals became a lot more toothsome.

Easter, our second in prison, came and passed with the same lack of events as any other day except for the religious services. But in another night, shortly after Easter, the entire prison was stirred awake by the whole body of Upper Prison warders and their Tanzanian co-keepers for head counts, with the usual, ritual harshness. That meant, as always, another escape.

Not quite. It turned out that some inmates at Soweto had prised open the door panel of their ward and managed to squeeze through the rather widely spaced burglar-proof bars. About ten of them were in the process of escaping but one who jumped down the wall first, broke his leg on impact and emitted a loud yell of distress, which brought the Tanzanians who had pitched camp nearby instantly awake. The rest, frozen in their tracks, heard him pleading for a *coup de grace*, which, according to them, the Tanzanians gave him straight from the barrel.

The rest of the would-be escapees, nearly caught red-handed, had to retreat post-haste to their ward. With the usual knee-jerk reaction, all the occupants of that ward were walloped hideously, then evicted and posted to other wards. That was probably the last loophole finally closed.

But, one might ask, what was the rationale behind always flogging the innocent ward mates, those who never attempted to escape? The prison warders argued that, in the first place, the measure was not essentially punitive or retaliatory; instead they meant to make the prisoners learn the hard way that they were their brothers' keepers; therefore they would be held accountable and blamed for the escape of a wardmate because it was their duty to report any prisoner in the process of escape. When some prisoners challenged them to explain how they could reach the authorities when they were under lock and key, they were told simply, "*Piga nduulu*", meaning "raise the alarm".

·····················

Towards the end of May, the president, marking the first anniversary of his return from exile, proclaimed the release of the prisoners "with immediate effect". That had to be definite and final. The president was showing goodwill. The prisoners' excitement could not be adequately described. That day our hair stylists had a heavy time again. Everyone was frantically preparing for departure the following day, according to the phrase "with immediate effect". Even the warders were convinced that was so, therefore, at their own discretion, they allowed us a whole day's spree in the sun to enable us to wash our clothes and carry out other preparations.

But days went by, so did weeks, a whole month and more, with not a sign of our departure whatsoever. Was that proclamation just another hoax? No. Rumour had it that the president really had the will to release the prisoners but he was not the sole arbiter of our fate and that there might be opposition or reluctance in certain extremist quarters of his Cabinet ranks; and that was perhaps what had caused him to be hesitant; even up until then, it seemed, our release was still in the moot stage or under consideration. The president's proclamation, however, was at least a promise—a debt. It was, therefore, still hoped that his will would prevail in the long run. But on the other hand, some come-lately prisoners were telling some of us that they had not expected to find us still alive. Out there, they said, there was a belief or suspicion that the prisoners might as well have been killed and that was why the release had not materialised in a long time since the president's proclamation. This speculation, as I learnt, was humorously based on the Luganda pun "okuta" and "okutta", which mean to release and to kill respectively. So the latter could have been the case, they thought, or perhaps liked to think.

As the days went by, our faith and hope based on that proclamation also began to wear out and yield to despair. But at last Radio Katwe predicted Monday 13th July, as the targeted date of our departure. That day also came and passed in vain; as usual we lost credence in our media once more. But ever hopeful and looking for favourable explanations, maybe the date was skipped because it involved an unlucky number. Instead, the following day, 14th July, brought us a visitor who by all accounts appeared to be laden with good tidings for us.

The bleak morning, with a haze, a drizzle and a cold draught, was rendered cheerful when we were all invited out onto the field. The visitor was an army subaltern, whom we found waiting for us and who was hob-nobbing with the newly-appointed commissioner as if they were peers of equal footing.

This uppity officer carried a file of papers under his arm, and when we had all gathered before him in defiance of the cold drizzle, he told us to listen attentively and to answer promptly to the names that were going to be read out; that if one was called, one had to rise at once and run, not just walk, to another designated position on the field.

There had never been such an urge, as there was now, to get out of prison. So this breathtaking event was, as it were, a foretaste of Judgment Day: There was so much nervousness, so much anxiety, so much attentiveness and so much silence that you could almost hear the heart palpitating from the next fellow! A clerk then began to read out the names, and the owners responded accordingly.

If you demurred or dawdled, our insolent visitor, no matter who you were, would bark at you in a manner and tone so hoity-toity, "Run, you shit, or I'll kick your ass!"

The selection, it turned out, was made exclusively from the regular servicemen, barring the Military Police and those who hailed from "areas infiltrated by bandits". Thus about 700 of us were segregated from the rest of the inmates, who from then on were denied contact with the out-goers and were sequestered to Soweto. The bisecting wall was now effectually an iron curtain. Undoubtedly, some of the inmates on the wrong side of it must have felt a wrench of the heart and lost consolation at the departure of their comrades. I did, however, manage to steal a parting word with one of them:

"The president understands the quality of mercy," I broached, half excited and half sorry for him.

"It's just as well you go and bell the cat for us who are staying behind," Colonel Mambo said, still as jolly as ever.

"How so?" I asked curiously.

Quoth Colonel Mambo, "If I hear that you people are being killed out there, then I'd rather stay put here; but if I hear that instead *you* people are the ones carrying out the killing, then I'll even apply for *habeas corpus*—in short order."

We laughed together for the last time.

Amin's Soldiers

CHAPTER TWELVE

FINAL DAYS

But, as a postscript, I should add:
"Never in the field of human conflict
was so much paid by so many for so few".

To paraphrase or, more precisely, counter-quote
Sir Winston (Leonard Spencer) Churchill.

THE FOLLOWING TEN DAYS were field days of hectic preparations occupied with taking photographs, fingerprints, heights and recording other particulars, presumably for the prison archives or as security precautions. Arrangements were also under way to facilitate our transportation to our respective districts using buses to be hired by the Government. Alongside, we were individually making ourselves ready for departure, with frenzied activity and alacrity.

The final days and nights seemed longer, as we waited for the day of departure, every moment filled with the happiest conversations and pleasantries. The superintendent himself, who had now become so popular with us, in informal discussions with some outgoers, shared in our happiness, even more so because he was going to have less of a headache with fewer mouths to feed. He cautioned, however, that, in the final analysis of crime and punishment, the paradox is that "imprisonment starts when you leave prison."

Expounding on this strange and cryptic contradiction, he said that he believed some of the outgoing prisoners were bound to find their homes gone to rack and ruin or desolate, with wives having deserted them or remarried, been made pregnant or already carrying new-born babies. Some of them might find their property all looted or expropriated. One way or another, a victim of such consequences would feel that he had been more sinned against than sinning. Might not such a man, supercharged with sheer emotional fury and despair, be motivated to kill and so bounce back to prison? Never mind the hard core habitual felons who kept endlessly rebounding to prison. In other words, imprisonment begets imprisonment.

"So, beware," the well-meaning superintendent cautioned.

The days progressed slowly, and the regime, although we were destined to be free men soon, never yielded even an ounce in its routine: head counts, lock-up and compulsory silence at bedtime were still enforced and observed as conscientiously as ever. It behoved us to keep toeing the line to the full, or else we could easily put paid to the prospect of our forthcoming release.

In that way we were now on good terms with all our keepers, who also cared to let us know that they wished us well. The preparations were over in about a week and we awaited the formalities. We would, so we were informed, be addressed by several Government functionaries before our departure.

The first to mount the rostrum was the Chief-of-Staff of the army, allegedly a blood relation to Obote, the man we had generally suspected (by mere prejudice, though) of being one of the devil's advocates against our release. He spoke of his exploits while in exile in Tanzania, as we listened with rapt attention and a grudging admiration of, not only a hero, but an invulnerable superman. Without mincing words, with a condescending manner and tone, he disclosed his intriguing, single-handed missions to disturb Idi Amin from time-to-time, which had eventually provoked Amin to invade Tanzania. That invasion had been a blessing in disguise because thereby they had at last found their *casus belli*. Hostilities were over and hatchets had been buried; they had nothing then against us. If they had wanted to kill us, they had had a golden opportunity to do so in the earliest stages of our confinement.

"What would we have gained by so doing? . . . Wouldn't that have been merely perpetuating the vicious circle, as revenge would beget revenge, and murder, murder?" he posed, rhetorically.

Then, coming to the crucial point, he said that we were about to be set free, but the army was not the only means of livelihood; we should go to our homes and be tillers of the earth; he would not like any of us prowling the town, or else he would give that person the hiding of his life. There was moderate laughter at that, and I deduced that was the chief's euphemism and pun to warn against going underground against their Government and what the grave consequences could be.

A grievance was then aired to him by a certain man who complained that he had been a would-be victim and, as a result, a deserter during Amin's regime. In his attempt to re-enlist in the new army, he had unfortunately been mis-routed to prison and had had to endure such agony again, whereas he should have been recompensed. "Moreover," he declared, raising his pitch amid general laughter, "I am a pure Langi!" He said that he had been, in a manner of speaking, married to the army man and boy; but what then was the reason for putting them asunder? What had happened to the proposition of returning to the army, his only vocation and his only hope?

"We are simply doing things in stages," the chief answered him. "Would you please go home and wait and see what will come later on."

But that enquiry illustrated the uncertainty and anxiety nearly all of us had about the future of our army career. Had the chief, by equivocating and parrying the question, served us with orders for our summary dismissal after all? So, although there was joy at leaving jail, some of us were lamenting too, for not going back to the army. Some prisoners, feeling demoralised, perhaps, might have been genuinely alienated from the army—to the point of disgust and contempt—whereas some others called it sour grapes.

The following morning came the Vice-President with a large entourage. His speech was a welcome note of atonement and conciliatory overtures, which we punctuated with several rounds of applause. There was the inevitable caution not to plot against the Government and to always be law-abiding citizens in our freedom to come.

"See for yourselves that the UPC Government has no intention to kill or victimise anyone. See for yourselves that the UPC is demonstrating the policy of no revenge. See for yourselves that UPC means well for you: In the name of God, tomorrow those doors will open wide for you," the Vice-President concluded, his voice rising with dramatic intonation. And what long, thunderous applause!

Then, as a postscript, he declared that the president had granted each outgoing prisoner a bounty of 2,000 shillings (to be sent to us after departure) as a token allowance towards rehabilitation. That was the icing on the cake, so we gave further resounding applause for that too, as he and his company got up and left.

On the Vice-President's word of honour, the following day, Saturday 25th July 1981, only 24 hours away, was to be our D-Day; our red letter day. Our excitement beggared description. We could now count down the hours. Would today were shorter, much shorter!

That afternoon our Red Cross patrons visited us for the last time and they supplied a bar of soap to each outgoer. They had also brought some more blankets, but as they were too few for our number, they had to be given out by drawing lots. That, the Bazungu said, was their contribution toward our resettlement.

The last supper was also generous and it tasted still better in our Seventh Heaven. The final night seemed longer than any other, in our sleeplessness and low-keyed or whispered conversations. At last, when the morning came, even the warder seemed to take too long to come and let us out for good, but come he eventually did.

We washed our faces in a frenzy and rinsed out our mouths, decked out ourselves in our finest clothes and stepped out of the miserable cells for the last time onto the field, where the others had already started assembling for the final briefing.

In a few minutes the Minister of Internal Affairs arrived accompanied by a large team of dignitaries. Some of them introduced themselves as members of Parliament as they took the platform in turns. They praised the merits of freedom, the happiness in being home with family and friends, but what a sad affair it would be if we went and abused the very freedom we had been pining for so much, by breaking the law and disrupting the peace and security!

Another of them pointed out (though not with such convincing argument) that the UPC Government, which was restoring our freedom, had played no part at all in our incarceration. Instead it had been the first and the second interim Governments of Lule and Binaisa who had been, in effect, our jailers, some of whose members were at the time actively hostile to the UPC Government, and who were, by ridiculous irony, hell bent on rescuing militarily the very prisoners they themselves had jailed. How magnanimous the president of UPC was!

The minister himself then closed with a caution that, whereas we were happy to leave jail, we were going to find life different and more challenging than ever, what with the recent gallop in inflation. We would find it hard to adjust to the new situation; but he could only wish us Godspeed. Then he pronounced a ritual incantation with a formula which goes something like: "By order of the President of the Republic of Uganda, you are free men. Go in peace!"

The final applause for the last speech was loud and protracted till the minister and his team were out of sight. The final hour had come. It was now left to the prison officers to implement the release order, and so, without loathing, they set to the process immediately and expeditiously. The number of outgoing prisoners, together with some more from Murchison Bay Prison, was 1,500 or thereabouts. We were released in groups of district origin, and it was sunset before the last batch of prisoners left the prison.

When our turn came, we were paid (typically and for subsistence for the long journey) 100 shillings each (peanuts!), given cyclo-styled gate passes and herded into the Reception Hall in the usual manner for the final head count before departure. When the formalities were over we were politely invited to step out of the prison quagmire and to head for the waiting bus.

Our orders were, "No glancing back."

And so at long last adieu Upper Prison.

Amin's Soldiers

EPILOGUE

AFTER OUR DEPARTURE, THE Government released another 3,000 prisoners or so—from Luzira Prison and other jails, in the course of the next two years. Big Baby and Colonel Enguli, as I learnt later, were released in the category "mental case" and posted to Butabika Mental Asylum, where they were "tamed", and from where they were eventually discharged.

Our protagonist, The Chieftain, was liberated amongst our lot and paid on departure a pittance of 300 shillings in appreciation of his headship over the prisoners. But the best luck, I have also heard, lay with one of our liberated cooks who had saved a sum from the food proceeds enough to enable him to buy cows for marrying a second wife, which is what he did!

There was never to be any formal general recall of Amin's soldiers back to the service after all. Most of them have since remained in Civvy Street—in the early years at least without meaningful employment, largely ignored by the state and in penury!

INDEX

A

absconding *63*
abundance *121, 124*
accommodation *22, 60*
Acholi *36–38*
Act of God *170*
administration block *44, 61*
advertising *66*
Air Force *34, 70*
alcoholism *77*
altercations *47*
ambassadors *32*
ambition *iv, 34, 39*
America *82, 119*
Amin, Idi *vii, x, 41, 141, 155, 178*
    Amin's criminal leadership *56*
    Amin's henchmen, etc. *54*
    Amin's misrule *27*
    Amin's soldiers *viii*
    anti-Amin exiles *x*
    banknotes *164*
    "gentle giant" *36*
    mass slaughter *38*
    spy network *85*
    unpopularity *37*
    unpredictability *37*
amnesty *20*
anaemia *106*
Angel Gabriel *112*
Anglican Archbishop *38, 135*
anonymity *xi*
anxiety *108, 129, 174, 179*
apartheid *49*
army *33*
    Army Jazz Band *138*
    recruiting *33*
arrogance *167*
Artful Dodgers *48*
Asians *37*
assassination
    assassination attempts *37*
    "assassination corner" *29*
assurances *20, 57, 90*
    Government assurances *20*
Astles, Bob *95*
atonement *179*

B

badinage *76*
Bald Heads *104*
Balokole *132*
banditry *101, 175*
bands *137, 138*
barbed wire *44*
barefoot *105*
basking in the sun *53*
batons *145*
Bazungu *81, 98, 115, 172, 180*
BBC News *165*
beans *48, 93, 115*

Amin's Soldiers

canned beans *75*
weevil-infested beans *48*
bedding *47, 69, 72, 81, 119, 154, 172*
Bedlam *161*
bedridden patients *51*
beer barons *65*
begging *97, 103, 109*
bewilderment *117*
Bible *81, 100, 112*
bicarbonate *107*
Big Baby *74, 97, 103, 116, 142, 183*
bigotry *50*
bigwigs *xi*
bilking *111*
Binaisa, Godfrey *82, 117, 119, 131, 155, 158*
bingo *81*
biscuits *159*
bistros *108, 121*
bitterness *109*
Black Hole of Kampala *21*
black market *105, 170, 171*
blackouts *68*
blankets *54, 69, 81, 95, 115, 161, 180*
blessing *129*
blood *171*
bookworms *166*
bootlegging *65, 73, 120, 125, 170*
booty *19, 39*
boredom *139*
"born-again" Christians *132*
bounty *121*
bracelets *68*
Brains Trust *50, 52, 95, 100, 139*
brainwashing *50*

brasshats *34*
brawls *47*
bribery *128, 159*
bric-a-brac *68*
Briefcase Man *153*
brinkmanship *38*
brotherhood *129*
brothers' keepers *173*
brutality *150*
brute force *52, 83*
buffoonery *viii, 137, 139*
Buganda *xvii, 21, 36, 82, 155, 158*
Buganda Kingdom *21*
bugging *122*
burglary *126*
businessmen *74, 75, 93, 120, 146*
business leagues *64*
business tycoons *32*
Butabika Mental Asylum *30, 183*

C

Cabinet *xi, 19, 38, 51, 82, 173*
callousness *106*
camaraderie *21*
campaign *115*
candies *64*
cane *83, 150*
canned food *64, 75, 147*
caprice *56*
Captain Mirinda *77, 110, 111, 134*
cards *100, 166*
care
intensive care *171*
carousing *40*

cassava *107*
cells *45, 65, 76, 94, 151, 180*
    punishment cell *127*
censorship *122, 165*
census *81, 113*
cereals *92*
ceremony *140*
chains *152*
chaplains *63*
charging *50*
    "Charging Ward" *96*
charisma *50, 155*
charity *119*
checkers *81, 100*
cheerlessness *106*
chess *103, 140*
Chief-of-Staff *56, 118, 178*
choir *111, 113, 124*
Christmas *111*
    Christmas play *141*
chronology *xi*
Churchill, Winston *50, 177*
cigarettes *64, 69, 103, 111, 149, 170*
cleansing agents *115*
clemency *156*
closed-circuit TV *44*
clothes *95, 119*
    hand-me-down clothes *172*
    threadbare clothes *105*
code
    coded messages *81*
    code of conduct *40*
    prison code *127*
coffee *66, 121, 170*
Cold War *37*

Colonel Enguli *30, 61, 96, 183*
Colonel Mambo *130, 137, 143, 149, 166, 170, 175*
comic relief *129*
commercial enterprise *64*
commissioner *87, 89, 101, 174*
    Commissioner of Prisons *22*
commodities *64*
complicity *165*
conciliation *156, 179*
concrete floors *69, 76*
condemnation *37*
Condemned Section *44, 95, 97*
confession *134*
confidence *23*
"confidentiality" *110*
confinement *56, 58, 154, 162*
congestion *47, 59, 62, 70, 153, 170*
conman *54, 148*
consequences *178*
consolation *115*
conspiracy *64, 106*
contraband *73, 148*
cooking pots *90*
cooks *72, 91, 113, 119, 150, 162, 183*
corporal punishment *52*
correction *52*
coup *35*
    coup attempts *37*
    coup d'etat *20*
courage *84*
courtyards *45, 85*
craftsmen *67*
credence *174*
crimes *58*

crime and punishment *177*
cruelty *145*, *150*
culinary delights *121*
curfew *21*, *28*, *141*, *153*

D

dance *138*
    folk dancing *139*, *142*
danger *25*, *49*, *60*, *114*, *157*, *161*
    dangerous criminals *60*
Dar es Salaam *38*, *155*, *156*
days of plenty *125*
deaths *106*
deficiency *106*
democracy *46*
demons *97*
dental caries *106*
derelict boat *45*, *72*, *90*
desertion *179*
desolation *139*
despondency *159*
detention *155*
    indefinite detention *156*
    "preventive detention" *39*
devil *93*, *135*, *156*
devotion *134*
diaries *163*
diarrhoea *107*
diet *85*, *118*
    meagre and monotonous diet *171*
    "penal diet" *127*
discipline *34*, *40*, *51*, *60*
disease *171*
dissidents *x*, *39*, *162*

distress *172*
district commissioners *32*
diversion *63*
documents *163*
dominoes *81*
Drake *32*
drama *111*
draughts *103*, *140*
drugs *115*, *171*
    over the counter drugs *64*
drum-driver *169*
drumming *63*
drunkenness *49*, *79*, *113*
dungeons *21*
dust *72*
dysentery *106*, *107*, *171*

E

elation *159*
elections *124*, *139*, *143*, *155*
    free and fair elections *19*, *158*
    postponement *156*
electricians *68*
elites *32*, *110*
    elitism *50*
emaciated figures *135*
emasculation *166*
emergency *49*, *156*, *170*
emotion *177*
endurance *47*
enguli *64*, *86*
ennui *166*
Entebbe *70*, *141*
    Entebbe Zoo *83*

raid on *vii*
envy *93, 168*
escape *44, 49, 63, 87, 106, 146, 152, 160, 172*
   Escapee Section *60*
escort *154*
ethnicity *139*
eucalyptus grove *91*
exaggeration *114*
executioner *65, 121, 148*
exercise *123, 149, 153*
exiles *38, 173, 178*
expendable *165*
expropriation *177*
extortion *148, 151*
extradition *32*
extravaganzas *137*
eyesight *106*

F

fabrication *54, 79, 84, 110*
faith *174*
false dawns *62*
family *53, 59, 81, 92, 115, 122*
   "lost" families *83*
   refugee families *81*
famine *167*
Fascism *39*
fate *54*
fatigue *166*
faultlessness *46*
fear *37, 86, 118, 155, 157*
feeble, senile men *51*
fencing *44*

feud
   internecine feuds *24*
fictions *111*
Fifth Column *38, 39*
fingerprints *177*
fire *170*
   fire and brimstone preacher *134*
firewood *66, 90, 121, 167*
flagellation *127*
flea markets *66*
flies *171*
   swarms of flies *154*
flogging *152, 160, 173*
flour *168*
folk-dancing *63*
folklore *28*
food *47, 90, 91, 107, 166*
   boost in supply *119*
   canned foods *83*
   food riots *49*
   mouldy food *171*
   shortages *168*
Fools' Paradise *55, 58, 59, 81, 110, 132, 134, 136*
football *81, 100, 113, 142*
forked tongues *156*
former ministers *32*
fortress *44*
fortune-tellers *59*
freedom *46, 57, 102, 108, 117, 180*
   freedom of expression *159*
French *124*
   French fries *121*
fried eggs *121*
friendship *129*

frog dance *34*
fruit *83*
frustration *65, 106*
fuel *94, 119, 167*
fugitive *19*
funeral atmosphere *84*
furniture *53, 66*

G

gallows-birds *107*
gambling *66, 72*
games *81, 100, 113, 166*
garbage *66, 96, 115, 119*
    filthy garbage *171*
garbage truck *62*
gate *44, 75, 117*
    gate passes *89, 112, 181*
genocide *36*
gentle giant *36*
ghee *172*
ghetto *69*
gin *65*
God *117, 132, 135, 136, 170*
    Act of God *170*
    ungodly deeds *134*
going home *136*
good
    good and bad tidings *82, 111, 174*
    good luck *59*
    good news *87*
    Good Samaritan *81*
goons *19*
Gospel according to Mammon *92*
gossip *73*

graffiti *61*
grapevine *82, 83*
greasing palms *63*
greed *93*
Grey Heads *104*
grudges *36*
grumbling *168*
guerrillas *40*
guilt *58*
    collective guilt *39*
gun *27, 49, 82, 91, 116, 120, 161*

H

habeas corpus *85, 175*
habitual felons *178*
Haji What's-'is-Name *89*
halitosis *119*
happiness *54, 180*
hardships *54, 56*
hats *68*
head counts *46, 63, 149, 160, 172, 178, 181*
health *27*
    health-promoting activity *123*
heartbreak *143*
henchmen *27, 54*
hoax *173*
hog *120*
hollow promise *19*
holocaust *38*
homesickness *54*
homilies *132*
hooliganism *49*
hope *54, 57, 81, 110, 136, 159, 174*
    false hope *19*

hospital *45, 53, 73, 86, 106, 107, 115, 120, 127, 154, 163, 171*
hospitality *121*
"houndmanship" *146*
hue and cry *30*
human
    humanitarian considerations *64, 83*
    human rights *46, 101*
    human slaughter *36*
humiliation *109, 150, 151, 163*
hunger *57, 72, 81, 90, 91, 96, 103, 162*
    hunger pangs *47*
hygiene *48, 115, 154*

I

identity
    identity papers *21, 163*
impresarios *138*
imprisonment *24, 177, 178*
incense *77*
inconsistency *58*
industry *67*
informers *165*
    counter-informers *165*
innocence *46*
insanity *151*
insecticides *115*
institutionalisation *158*
insurrection *36, 38*
intimacy *62*
invalids *51*
"iron rations" *110*
Israelis *34*

J

jazz
    Army Jazz Band *138*
Jesus Christ *152*
John Bull *32*
Judgment Day *174*
juniors *49*
justice *114*

K

Kabaka Mutesa II *33*
Kampala *19, 90, 141*
    fall of Kampala *41*
kangaroo court *50*
kanzu *137*
Karimojong *34*
Katwe *54*
keepers *83, 87*
Kenya *32*
Kiganda *103*
killing *174, 175*
    "overkilling" *143*
    wanton killing *x*
King Herod *112*
King Mutesa II *21*
kitchens *44, 47, 51, 52, 108, 119, 162*
    kitchen police *169*
kith and kin *83, 137, 155*

L

labour *46*
Lake Victoria *43, 70*

Langi *36*
laundry *44*
laxity *120*
leniency *41, 120*
lethargy *166*
letters *81, 115, 163*
liberation *19, 39*
liberty *148, 166*
library *163, 166*
Libya *viii*
lice *26, 56, 72, 105, 154*
lies *54, 55, 61, 78*
liquor *97, 148, 150*
lock-up *149, 153, 178*
lodgers *51*
logging *91*
loofahs *68*
looting *52, 53, 68, 69, 97, 177*
love *82, 119*
loyalty *19*
Lubiri *33*
Ludo *81, 100*
Luganda *74, 113*
Lugard's soldier *30, 69, 117*
Lule, Yusef *19, 82*
Luzira Prison *22, 25, 43, 119, 145, 183*
lynchings *19, 58*

M

madaraka *154*
maggots *107, 120*
maize *107, 119, 167*
Makindye Military Prison *20, 21*
    Makindye Barracks *139*

malady *106*
malcontents *163*
male chauvinism *74*
malice *24*
Maroons *100*
matches *170*
matoke *92, 121*
mats *68*
meals
    meagre meals *22*
meat *92*
medicine *73, 106, 171*
mental health *106, 183*
merchandising *66*
mercy *xii, 89, 111, 175*
    small mercies *117*
merriment *64, 143*
Michelin Man (Major Michelin) *28, 105, 122*
MiG 21 jet fighters *38*
migraine *106*
military
    Military Commission *116, 118, 155, 158*
    military tradition *45*
    military upbringing *50*
    military uprising *xi*
milk-powder *115, 159*
Minister of Defence *58*
Minister of Internal Affairs *57, 63, 88*
Ministry of Internal Affairs *85, 101*
modesty *163*
Mogadishu *37*
Molotov cocktails *146*
money *119, 121, 146, 147, 150, 159*

Index

morale *21, 101*
morality *129*
Moroto *34*
Moshi *24, 39, 158*
motivation *51*
Muganda *xvii, 139, 158*
Mulago *106*
  Mulago Hospital *106*
Murchison Bay Prison *47, 100, 181*
murderous deeds *89*
music *124, 138*
  musical chairs *60*
Muslims *120, 121, 153*
mutiny *49, 157, 162*
Muwanga, Paulo *158*
Mzekobe *31, 51*

N

naïvety *46, 159*
Nakasongola *39*
National Consultative Council *19*
Nativity play *111*
necklaces *68*
needs *56*
nepotism *89*
nervousness *174*
neurosis *108*
news *122, 154*
  newspapers *54, 85, 89, 101*
niggardliness *107*
nostalgia *70, 138*
Nubians *31*
nuisance *97*
"Nuremberg Trials" *115*

nurses *73, 74, 120*
Nyerere, Julius *37, 156*
  "Nyerere's Bay of Pigs" *37*

O

Obote, Milton *xi, 35, 155*
obsessions *107*
officers *93*
  officers' wing *97, 109*
old wives' tales *28*
olive branch *20*
Oliver Twists *48*
oppression *x*
optimism *109*
oracles *59*
ordeal *81*
ostracism *95*
outlaws *95*
overcrowding *69, 148*

P

panic *84, 161*
paramilitaries *32*
paranoia *38*
parasites *72*
pardon *139*
pastries *64*
patience *158*
peace *19, 181*
  peace of mind *161*
  peace pact *37*
peanuts *64, 73, 75*
penitence *134*

193

performances *137*
perks *51*
permanent secretaries *32*
pernicious regime *105*
photographs *177*
physical education *124*
pickpockets *95*
pillory
    being pilloried *83*
    pillory-like structure *127*
pins and needles *166*
planes *35*
playground *69, 74*
playing cards *81*
plays *139*
plunder *x*
police *33, 54, 101*
    arrest of *29*
    kitchen police *52*
    Military Police *175*
politics *129*
    political bickering *130*
    political intimidation *x*
    politicians *19*
pomp *140*
Pontius Pilate *117*
porridge *66, 91, 107*
potatoes *92*
    rotten potatoes *96*
power *24*
    power-hungry scrambles *158*
prayer *69, 134, 161*
    orgies of praying *132*
precedent *114*
predictions *55*

prejudice *155*
presidency *x*
prevarication *106*
preventive detention *39*
prison *24, 29, 43, 70*
    all level in prison *52*
    fewer jails the better *70*
    prison archives *177*
    prison break *157*
    Prison Mess *137*
    Prison Superintendent *51*
prisoners
    prisoners-of-war *87, 112*
    sick prisoners *154*
privacy *61*
privations *22*
privileges *83, 126, 166, 169*
procedures *63*
proclamation *173*
profiteering *93*
promiscuity *95*
promises *158*
pronouncements *55, 160, 181*
provincial governors *32*
provisioner *107*
psychological disorders *106*
publicans *76*
Public Security Unit *101*
pugilism *124*
punishment cells *44*
putsch *35*

R

rackets *65*

radar *40*
radio *75, 82, 112, 159*
    portable radio *165*
    Radio Deutsche Welle *141*
    Radio Katwe *54, 62, 174*
    Radio Uganda *54*
Ramadhan *120*
ransacking *146*
ransom *159*
rations *127, 169*
reading *81*
reassurances *22, 159*
rebellion
    rebel movements *159*
    seeds of rebellion *156*
reception *70*
    visitors' reception *122*
Reconstruction, Rehabilitation, Reconciliation *19*
records *177*
recreation *53*
recruiting *33*
Red Cross *xii, 55, 81, 115, 159, 166, 171, 180*
redemption *163*
refuse *62, 72*
rehabilitation *179*
release *54, 70, 83, 85, 101, 115, 130, 178*
    Christmas release *111*
relief *81*
religion *143*
    religious leaders visit prison *135*
repression *127*
resentment *93*
resettlement *180*

respect *50, 140, 167*
restraint *127, 166*
restrictions *141, 148*
retailers *65, 73*
    furtive retailing *170*
retribution *24, 94*
revenge *24, 156*
Reverend Sisters *69*
rice *115, 121*
rights *46, 106*
rings *68*
Riot Act *84, 127*
risk *153*
ritual *181*
robbery *101*
Robinson Crusoe *105*
robots *164*
roll call *51*
"rolling stroll" *53*
routine *63*
rumour *28, 57, 62, 72, 81, 108, 122, 132, 173*
    butchering *84*
    "Radio Katwe" *54*
    rumour mill *54*
runaway inflation *63, 65*
ruses *164*

S

sabre-rattling *38*
sackcloth *68*
sadism *150*
safety *165*
salad days *68, 166*

salt *64, 83*
salvation *159*
sanctuary *32, 37, 151*
Sandhurst *130*
Satan *134*
satchels *68*
Saudi Arabia *viii*
scales *106*
scolding *126*
scorched-earth policy *39*
Scrabble *75, 81, 100, 109, 130*
scrambling *95, 109*
    scrambling for food *48*
screening exercise *57*
seamsters *67*
search *111, 146, 150, 163*
    random searches *163*
    superficial searches *125*
security *19, 27, 155, 167*
    maximum security *35, 43*
    security precautions *177*
seeing stars *109*
self
    self-control *51*
    self-defence *123*
    self-government *51*
    self-righteousness *134*
sex-starved inmates *73*
shakedowns *147*
shame *19*
shanties *43*
shoe repairers *67*
shooting *86*
shortages *37*
showers *45, 61, 69, 73, 98, 153*

sick bay *106*
silence *178*
siren *153*
sisal *68*
sleep *65, 80, 81, 167*
slogans *22*
slugabed *69*
smells *153*
smoked fish *115*
smuggling *64, 91, 120, 165, 170*
smugness *167*
Snakes and Ladders *100*
snitching *165*
soap *64, 83, 99, 105, 115, 163, 172, 180*
social justice *19*
Sodom and Gomorrha *142*
solace *54, 85, 136*
solitary confinement *127*
Somalia *37*
South Africa *49*
"Soweto" *49, 64, 66, 69, 72, 76, 86, 96, 121,*
    140, 154, 172, 175
Spartan fare *47*
spies *85, 165*
spoils *53, 146*
sport *148*
    Sports Committee *100, 139*
squalor *115, 154*
staff training college *43*
stale urine *62*
starvation *107, 119*
State Research Bureau *85*
stationery *64, 81, 115, 163*
stench *153*
stigma *xi*

stir-crazy *106*
stoicism *47*
streaking *74*
strife *xi*
strong-arm tactics *50*
students *32*
stunts *139*
subversion *89, 122*
Sudanese Foreign Legion *155*
suffering *163*
sugar *64, 67, 72, 75, 83, 115, 159*
suicide *20*
sunshine *69*
superintendent *52, 55, 60, 62, 66, 83, 94, 114, 126, 171, 177*
superstition *59, 134*
surrender *20*
surveillance *44*
survival *37, 57, 168*
    survival of the richest *159*
suspense *103*
suspicion *24, 37, 155, 156*
swagger sticks *49*
Sword of Damocles *38*
sympathy *171*

T

taarab *xvii, 142*
taekwondo *123*
"tank bistros" *72*
tanks *82*
Tanzania *27, 30*
    Tanzanian guards *146*
    Tanzanian hegemony *118*
    Tanzanian soldiers *49*
    Tanzanian Supreme Command *90*
    Tanzania People's Defence Force *x, 39*
    Uganda-Tanzania hostilities *37*
tax collector *164*
tea *66, 72, 109*
    "high tea" *160*
    tea-and-toast *90, 120, 153, 167*
temporising tactics *115*
temptation *92*
"ten cells" system *21*
terror
    reign of terror *37*
The Battle *140*
The Chieftain *50, 58, 74, 91, 104, 108, 126, 140, 150, 166, 168, 183*
theft *95, 126, 128*
    "Thieves' Ward" *95*
The Shirts *104*
The Skins *104*
thrashing *151*
tinkers *68*
tinsmiths *68*
toeing the line *178*
toilet *45, 61, 152, 160*
    clogged toilets *171*
    toilet paper *115*
tools *165*
    "tools of a murderous reign" *165*
toothpaste *105*
    toothpaste tubes *163*
torture *150*
tradition *29, 33, 103, 137*
transport *167*
treason *162, 166*

tribes *19, 36, 37, 139, 158*
trouble-shooters *52*
truncheons *25*
trust *57, 78, 163*
    distrust *24*
turkey *121*
turnkeys *64*
typhoid fever *172*
tyranny *151*

U

ugali 26, 46, 48, 75, 96, 163
Uganda
    Ugandan Air Force *34, 70*
    Uganda National Liberation Army *56*
    Uganda National Liberation Front *x, 19, 39*
unburdening the cross *129*
uncertainty *159, 179*
underground *178*
underworld *54*
unga xvii, 108, 115
ungali 115
uniforms
    abandoned uniforms *22*
Upper Prison *25, 27, 35, 43*
utensils *66, 101, 146*
Utopia *19*

V

vagueness *160*
variety shows *139*
vegetable *46*

vegetable life *81*
vengeance *20, 24*
ventilation *69*
vermin *28, 171*
victim *24, 57, 60, 177, 179*
    victimisation *19*
vigilance *84*
visitors *83, 117, 122, 139, 156*
    banned *84, 143*
    visitors' reception room *83*
volleyball *45, 81, 103, 113, 140*

W

want *54, 95, 109*
wanted *85*
    wanted criminals *60*
war *xi*
    spoils of war *19*
warders *53, 61, 145*
    subornation of *165*
wards *69, 95, 124, 151*
    makeshift wards *60*
watchtower *44*
weapons *20, 40, 117*
weavers *68*
wedding gala *137*
Western media *36*
whipping *127, 151*
whispers *82*
wickedness *159*
wings *45, 61*
    officers' wing *75, 85*
witchcraft *134*
    witch-hunt *21*

woes *54*
wood cutters *169*
Wooden Horse *63*
Word of God *132*
workshops *44, 53, 68*
worry *106*
wrestling matches *139*

Y

youths *49*

Z

zeal *25, 29, 52, 132*
    religious zeal *134*

Also from Waterside Press

Her Majesty's Philosophers
by Alan Smith

Informative, entertaining, against the grain, *Her Majesty's Philosophers* highlights the artificiality of prison life. By a *Guardian* correspondent, this book is set to be a penal affairs classic which every student of crime and punishment should read.

Building on his *Guardian* pieces about teaching Philosophy in prison, this is Alan Smith's account *in extenso*. From introducing Plato to ever-changing groups of hard-nosed prisoners to them wrestling with Bentham, Larkin and Shakespeare, it is packed with insights and unexpected turns. It paints a picture in which worlds collide and conventional morality is turned inside out as 'new modes of discourse' change the men's thinking and ideas. At times surreal the book brings fresh perspectives to the minutiae of prison life: survival, coping, soap, teabags, cell mates, the constant noise and immediacy. And needless to say, the men come up with philosophical gems of their own.

'Revealing, wry, provocative…': Amy Leavitt , Writer, USA.

'Alan Smith is…a master story-teller': Dick Gordon, *The Story*

'The author has never flinched from telling the vivid truth about prison: how it can mess with people's minds': Alice Woolley, *The Guardian*.

Paperback & Ebook | ISBN 978-1-904380-95-5 | 2013 | 216 pages

www.WatersidePress.co.uk

Also from Waterside Press

Dear Fiona
Letters from a Suspected Soviet Spy
by Fiona Fullerton

He was a suspected Cold War spy. She became the glamorous KGB double agent in a Bond movie. When a prisoner writes to a movie star, the best he can hope for is a signed photo. But when Alex wrote to Fiona she was beguiled by the artistry of his letters and poems. In this heartfelt memoir, the author recalls — for the first time — her 12 year correspondence with Prisoner 789959 Alexander Alexandrowicz — including his wise counsel about her marriage, divorce and career at the forefront of cinema, TV and theatre. Based on their original letters, the narrative is one of contrasts — about a man in the darkest days of prolonged incarceration and a woman surrounded by the brightest lights imaginable. Shocked by his long sentence, Alex protested his innocence and railed against the system, often from solitary confinement — whilst Fiona Fullerton roamed the world, a celebrity nomad.

'A poignant illustration of two different lives; both of whom lived existences that most people can only read about in the red tops. It is a book that I shall keep on my bookshelf and read again, high praise indeed': *Inside Time.*

'Wonderful, fascinating, fantastic': Aled Jones, Good Morning Sunday, BBC Radio 2.

'Compelling, gripping, moving, insightful': Erwin James, *Guardian* correspondent.

'Makes for compulsive reading': Edward Fitzgerald CBE QC

Hardback & Ebook | ISBN 978-1-904380-85-6 | 2012 | 304 pages + 16 picture pages

www.ingramcontent.com/pod-product-compliance
Lightning Source LLC
Chambersburg PA
CBHW051126160426
43195CB00014B/2358